INEQUAL
EVOLUTION

MW00891678

INEQUALITY AND EVOLUTION

The Biological Determinants
of Capitalism, Socialism and
Income Inequality

Charles L. Ladner

To order additional copies of this book, contact:
Xlibris
844-714-8691
www.Xlibris.com
Orders@Xlibris.com
819169

CONTENTS

Preface xi

Introduction...xvii

Part 1: The Biological Imperative

Chapter 1: Evolution 1
    The Struggle for Life 1
    Natural Selection...3
    The Neo-Darwinian Synthesis....................................5

Chapter 2: The Cell, DNA, Genes, and Selfish Behavior..................8
    The Similarity of Plants and Animals 8
    Chromosomes, DNA, and Genes: The Seat of
        Selfish Behavior?...10
    The Search for the Origin of Selfish Behavior.......12
    The Elusive Mystery of Scale...................................14

Chapter 3: Socialization 19
    The First Derivative of Selfishness..........................19

Part 2: The Economic Systems

Chapter 4: Setting the Scene 27
    The Influence of Genetic Instincts on the Economic
        Behavior of Early Humans 29
    The Egyptian Model 31
    The Roman Model...34

Chapter 5: Aids to Analysis: Income and Inequality Data 40

Chapter 6: Socialism 45
  The Creation of the World's First and Most Successful
    Socialist State: The Union of Soviet Socialist Republics ...49

Chapter 7: The Collapse of the Soviet Union 53

Chapter 8: Lessons regarding the Viability of Socialism.................62
  Socialism in China: Been There, Done That!.......................66

Chapter 9: Capitalism and Free Enterprise 69

Chapter 10: Types of Capitalism: Liberal Meritocratic Capitalism ...80
  The Development of Twentieth-Century Social
    Democratic Capitalism...81
  The Emergence of Liberal Meritocratic Capitalism..............85

Chapter 11: Types of Capitalism: Political Capitalism 100
  China: The Archetype of Political Capitalism.....................100
  Who Is Xi Jinping?..109
  Where Is Xi Jinping and the Communist Party
    Taking China? 112

Chapter 12: Wither Capitalism: Can It Continue as the Sole
    Source of Prosperity, or Will It Capitulate to Its
    Own Self-Destructive Tendencies? 118
  The Inherent Contradictions of Capitalism..........................121
  Income and Wealth Inequality..124
  The Justification for Gradations in Income 129
  An Analysis of the Inequality Problem in the United States ...131
  A Pragmatic Solution 142
  A Generalized Proposal for Increased Income Taxes to
    the 1% 144
  Taxation of Wealth 148

Chapter 13: Conclusion...154
    Evolution 158

Appendix A...161
Appendix B...167
Acknowledgments 169
Bibliography...171
Index...181

LIST OF FIGURES AND TABLES

List of Figures

Figure 1. Plant versus Animal Cell 9
Figure 2. Income and Wealth: Top 0.1% 1915–2012 98
Figure 3. Increase in Annual Income after Tax and Transfers
for 2016 over 1979 by Quintile and the Top 1%...........................136

List of Tables

Table 1. Inequality in Ancient Rome 38
Table 2. Income and Inequality Data for Selected Countries...........43
Table 3. Percent Distribution of Personal Income by Quintile 44
Table 4. Gross Domestic Product Per Capita (PPP) of Selected
          Socialist and Former Socialist Countries 1950–2016 77
Table 5. Gross Domestic Product Per Capita of Selected
          Socialist and Former Socialist Countries as a Percent
          of the United States 1950–2016...78
Table 6. Regional GDP Per Capita, Regional Growth in GDP
          Per Capita, the Percent of the United States GDP Per
          Capita 1990–2018 84
Table 7. Key Features of Classical, Social Democratic, and
          Liberal Meritocratic Capitalism (from Milanovic′) 91
Table 8. Thresholds and Shares in Top Wealth Groups, 2012 93
Table 9. Percent of National Income by Income Group 95
Table 10. Attribution of Increased Income from Change in Share ...96
Table 11. Share of Transactions Conducted at Market Prices 102
Table 12. US Household Income and Gini Coefficients
          1979–2016 126
Table 13. Income after Tax and Transfer 1979–2016 133

Table 14. Income after Tax and Transfer 1979–2016 at the
    GDP/Capita Thirty-Seven-Year Compound Annual
    Growth Rate of 1.45% 135
Table 15. Deconstruction of the Top Quintile Income for 2016.....140
Table 16. Pro Forma Deconstruction of the Top Quintile
    Income for 2016 with Income Tax Changes to
    Produce a .306 Gini for All Quintiles and a Uniform
    1.45% CAGR for All Quintiles from 1979 143
Table 17. Pro Forma Deconstruction of the Top Quintile
    Income for 2016 with Pragmatic Changes in Income
    Taxes...145
Table 18. The Net Redistributive Effect on Income Inequality
    from Increased Income and Wealth Taxes on the Top
    1% with All Benefits Allocated to the Middle Class
    (Quintiles 2–4) 151
Table 19. The Net Redistributive Effect on Income Inequality
    from Increased Income and Wealth Taxes on the Top
    1% with Benefits Allocated to All but the Top Quintile 152

PREFACE

THE 2020 PRESIDENTIAL election revealed a serious fracturing of the American electorate. Donald Trump, himself, was clearly rejected. But the widespread discontent, first exposed by his election in 2016, again manifested itself with a significant voter preference for the alternative policies he originally embraced. There was no "blue wave' as had been expected, and it now seems perfectly clear that there is a substantial segment of the nation, perhaps as much as half, who believe they are left out, have fallen behind, and are resentful of those who appear to be unfairly benefitting by today's society and its attendant economic direction. These people comprise the great American working class, those who in statistical terms, fall within second, third and fourth quintiles of income distribution.

This book, *Inequality and Evolution*, explains the origins of this discontent, why it is justifiable, why it will not fade away, and how to fix it.

The root of the matter, that is to say the source of middle class discontent, is the quite accurate perception that the distribution of societal benefits in the form of income after taxes and government transfers (social security and welfare), has become grossly unfair. In this book, it is demonstrated by an analysis of household income that shows that federal income tax and other government programs since the 1980's, have been consistently oriented towards advantaging the top and bottom income quintiles at the expense of the middle quintiles. In fact, if the income of all classes had advanced proportionately over the period 1979-2016 at the same rate of growth (CAGR 1.45%), the middle class annual income in 2016 would have been about $860 billion more than it was, while the bottom quintile would have been $2 billion less, and the top 1% about $857 billion less. Said differently and more graphically, for the year 2016, the cumulative effect of biased tax and governmental policies since 1980, has produced a condition whereby the average middle class household contributed about $11,500 in reduced annual income, so that the average upper class household of those in the top 1% could enjoy about $685 thousand in increased annual income.

This issue of inequality and a proposed solution are taken up in the last two chapters of the book. They are supported by the main body of the work comprising the eleven preceding chapters in which there is constructed an economic analysis grounded in evolutionary biology.

My principal thesis is that the biological need for survival and reproduction undergirding the theory of Evolution, and specifically constituting the operative principle of Natural Selection, is the main force that determines economic behavior. This drive for survival and reproduction is expressed in humans by a variety of strategies and actions which I encapsulate under the term: selfishness.

I will further argue that the success or failure of an economic system is wholly dependent on the degree to which it allows this primal need to be expressed. Thus, when embodied in the state, socialism (i.e., state socialism) will always fail because its implementation requires an authoritarian rule that acts to suppress individual selfishness, while capitalism, which is grounded in the expression of selfishness (or greed), will always prevail.

However, regarding capitalism, there is one caveat. And that has to do with its propensity to produce inequality in income and wealth. I maintain that while this dynamic provides the aspirational energy that makes capitalism so successful, if it is not restrained, it can cause a capitalist system to self-destruct through the combination of environmental despoliation, monopoly, and concentration of wealth. I will address these matters, especially the question of inequality in the United States, in the concluding chapters of this book.

There are a few quantitative concepts used in the book that may not be familiar to most people, so I would like to offer some explanations that should make it easier to understand.

Constant dollars. All time series data is presented in constant dollars to take out the effect of inflation. For example, $1.00 in 1979 is equivalent to $3.31 in 2016. Therefore, to isolate economic growth without the effect of inflation, a 1979 dollar is increased to $3.31.

Purchasing power parity. In addition to inflation, economic comparisons among regions and countries can be distorted by the cost of goods and services in one country versus the cost of goods and services in another country. Recognizing this matter, economists typically convert all values to a single benchmark currency and then adjust the values in any given year for the relative costs of goods and services (including wage rates) to that of the benchmark country. When making comparisons among countries, I prefer the World Bank data, which uses the United States as the benchmark country and 2017 as the constant dollar year.

Sources: different datasets. In recent years, a number of economists throughout the world have been developing increasingly broad and precise datasets to analyze national and regional income and wealth characteristics over varying time periods. Within each dataset, there is consistency; but among datasets, there are variations arising from different wealth concepts and measurements over different frequencies or time periods. I have used different datasets throughout this book to take advantage of their relative strengths where appropriate to the topic under discussion. In each case, I have clearly identified the source.

Tables versus graphs. In most books that address current economic topics, the use of both line and bar graphs has become quite common— and for good reason: the visualization of economic trends and their possible range of extrapolative values are typically better communicated by a line graph than by a series of numbers. Numbers imply precision, while a graph can leave open varying interpretations. In this work, however, I believe that tables can convey the information more effectively, especially as in chapter 12, where a common format is used to describe events over different time periods and within different subgroups.

Per capita GDP versus total GDP. In most cases (though not all), when_making comparisons between countries or between different time periods, it is useful to express the data using a common denominator. In this work, there are numerous comparisons of gross domestic product (GDP) between countries and over various time periods where the use of total GDP would be misleading but where the use of per capita GDP is the only way to accurately convey meaning.

To the extent possible, all references in this book are to GDP expressed on a per capita basis.

CAGR (compound annual growth rate). This is one of the many ways to describe the rate of growth. While typically the growth of a factor (like GDP) over time is expressed as either an average rate of growth or as the percent change from the starting point to the end point, the CAGR is the *compound* rate of growth. It's like bond interest. The advantage of CAGR is that it eliminates the effect of wide year-to-year positive and negative swings that can otherwise distort an arithmetic average. To understand the compounding effect, it is useful to remember that if something grows at a 7% CAGR, it will double in ten years. It also should be noted that every use of CAGR in this book is applied to constant dollars, so in the tables, CAGR is the growth over and above inflation.

Finally, in the last few chapters where I address the question of income and wealth inequality in the United States, I use 1979 as the benchmark year against which to measure current levels of inequality. I use 1979 because it was the last year of a three-decade period that represented the most equitable period of income and wealth distribution during the twentieth century and perhaps even the entire history of European settlement in what is now the United States.

In 1929, the top one-tenth of 1% of the population (0.01%) accounted for almost 8% of the national income. Over the next two decades, spanning the Depression years and World War II, this percentage fell to about 3%, where it remained until 1980. It began a steep rise back to 8%. This is well illustrated by figure 2 on page 128. Many people feel that in terms of economic justice, the period bounded by 1945 to 1980 was a golden age when high economic growth was accompanied by an equitable distribution of income. However, there was one blot on the landscape, and that was the very poor situation of the bottom quintile. In the 1960s, the conscience of the nation was pricked and thus followed the Great Society programs aimed at eliminating poverty and racial injustice. By 1979, the full effect of these programs was visible. The income of the bottom quintile was doubled after including taxes and federal transfer programs, while the net effect for other income classes was negligible. Therefore, in my view, when considering both growth and inequality, the late 1970s represented the best of all times, a worthy goal for policymakers, and the correct benchmark for analysis.

INTRODUCTION

WHEN STRUGGLING WITH a complex problem, many people find the solution by reducing the matter to its most simple elements. They eliminate all the ambiguity and focus solely on the fundamental part of the question. I know this is what I do. In fact, I would go so far as to say that in nearly every case, I find simplicity to be the best and, perhaps, the only way to find an acceptable answer.

There is nothing original about this approach. It's been around since the Middle Ages in the form of a logical principle commonly known as Occam's razor. For our purposes, I would like to point out that this procedure, "shaving away" the incidentals, is exactly what I will be doing in this study, where the object is to analyze two complex economic systems—capitalism and socialism—through the lens of the biological force that produces evolutionary natural selection. This force is common to all living things—plants, animals, insects, fish, and even lichen. In fact, according to evolutionary biologists, it is that that makes life itself possible on earth.[1] Absent this factor, our planet would be a cold, near-lifeless body drifting in space, populated, at best, by colonies of bacteria and probably not even that.

It may be hard for anyone to see any connection between an ordinary human motivation and the existence of life. It may appear even more absurd because what I am describing is nothing more than the simple biological need for survival and reproduction or, said differently and summarized in a single word, *selfishness*. Once having trimmed away all the complexities and incidentals of a human social organization or economic structure, what remains is its fundamental driving force, and it is selfishness that lies at the heart of such systems, as it does for all other expressions of organized human behavior.

---

1   This statement appears outrageous, but it is not, as will become perfectly clear in the discussion of Darwin's theory of natural selection.

The science of evolution identifies survival and reproduction as the most fundamental requirement of life. It is that without which life cannot exist. Together, the need for survival and reproduction is expressed by the living organism in a variety of actions and strategies, which I describe as selfishness. However, even though I will stay with the term *selfishness* throughout this book, in the context of economics, one could also use the more limited and less comprehensive word *greed*.

In high school biology, we learned that this basic drive—intrinsic to all living things, from plants to animals, including even insects and bacteria—is the will to survive and the push to reproduce. Apart from these two intrinsic needs, all other motivations are secondary. Only the will for survival and reproduction is uniformly common among all living things. Other motivations, say for example, Freudian compulsions in humans, will certainly arise, but only sporadically and only in people where unconscious behavior or reasoned notions of conscience, morality, and empathy can temporarily overcome the fundamental force of selfishness that constitutes the first principle of life and evolution.

So well accepted is the primacy of the need for survival and reproduction intrinsic to our nature that in texts beyond elementary biology, it is taken for granted and infrequently mentioned. On the other hand, within scholarly circles, there is an almost obsessive amount of attention paid to the genetic or social origins of altruism. Why? Because within the universe of living things, where selfishness rules, altruism is both rare and contrary to the rule of life, typically construed as a means to assure survival by cooperative group action. But we should note that altruism, or the herding instinct or the propensity for some creatures to live in cooperative colonies, are genetic adaptations to the overriding requirement to preserve and reproduce life. They are a means to the end; the end being survival and reproduction.

This study, while ostensibly a work of economics, begins by reducing economic questions to their simplest elements, the primary motivations that compel man to economic action. Thus, this book is centered on biological predispositions of survival and reproduction (i.e., selfishness) insofar as they influence the human individual and group behaviors.

Following upon these findings, I will be examining the principal economic and political theories (i.e., socialism and capitalism) that are presently in the forefront of public discussion. I will be doing this through an evolutionary and genetic lens.

We know that the primary force of survival and reproduction runs in an uninterrupted causal relationship, beginning with the first appearance of life on earth and flowing through its every manifestation from single-cell prokaryotes through plants, insects, mammals, and up and including humankind. Therefore, it is my thesis that economic behavior—that is to say, the process by which humans obtain food, shelter, self-defense, and the necessities of life—is nothing more than the crystallization of these primary needs in everyday life and that all economic behavior can be thus explained.

The first three chapters in this book are brief historical reviews of the development of evolutionary theory, its elaboration in cellular biology, and its further expression in biologically derived socialization. In this study, evolution is seen as the general condition, a design or formal cause, by which all of nature proceeds; while genetics, a subset of cellular biology, is the active principle, the instrument or efficient cause, of evolutionary activity and of socialization, which is its primary learned response among humans.

The fourth chapter is an overview of the more primitive means by which humans organized economic activity, beginning with early tribal economies and culminating in the nascent emergence of a free market semicapitalist system within the Roman Empire. By the late sixth century CE, both in the Eastern Empire and within the chaotic remnants of the Western Empire, the disintegration of civic order resulted in the development of the feudal system of economic organization that remained, more or less, intact until the reemergence of long-distance trading and free markets, which, in the West, began to appear in the Netherlands and England in the sixteenth century.

The fifth chapter is an introduction to some of the analytical tools that will be used throughout the remainder of the book.

The next four chapters move to the nineteenth, twentieth, and twenty-first centuries with discussions of socialism and capitalism. However, I should point out that when I refer to socialism as a system, I am not referring to individual social programs within, for example, a capitalist system that are commonly (and sometimes pejoratively) labeled as socialism; but rather, I am referring to socialism when considered as the exclusive organizing principle of a nation's economy—in other words, state socialism, such as that found in Russia during the 1917–1991 period. Finally, the concluding chapters are an analysis of the self-destructive tendencies emerging in present-day capitalism in the United States, along with suggestions for corrective action that will enable the system to prevail.

Throughout this book, the Darwinian notion of selfishness underlying the theory of natural selection is shown to be operative in even the most complex and sophisticated human activity. From this flows the key finding that the determinism embodied in human selfishness causes authoritarian systems, such as socialism, to always fail, while it causes more liberal systems, such as capitalism, to always flourish (up to the point where they, too, become illiberal). And the unanswered question is whether capitalism can be structured to contain its internal tendency toward such self-annihilation by overreach.

The foundational concept on which Darwin and subsequent evolutionary biologists based the whole theory of evolution is that of embedded selfishness. Absent selfishness, there is no natural selection; and absent natural selection, there is no evolution. These truths influence all life, from the simplest single-cell prokaryote to plants and to humans, the most complex of all living organisms. So in studying the behavior of the human organism, including economic behavior, it is important to get a feel of the underlying science. The science of evolution, like all great ideas, is not difficult to comprehend. What makes it appear so and what impeded humankind from having developed such a theory at an earlier period was, first of all, conflicting interpretations of the Judeo-Christian scriptures that had dominated intellectual thought for two millennia and, secondly, a disdain for empirical and experimental logic.

Evolution, in the near-poetic words of Jesuit paleontologist and theologian Pierre Teilhard de Chardin, "is a light illuminating all facts, a curve that all lines must follow."[2] Teilhard was speaking mainly about theological matters, but I am convinced that his insight is equally applicable to nearly all spheres of human social activity and not just limited to the domains of biology or religion. I will hope to show that the genetic imperative that triggers the Darwinian response in individuals and species also critically influences, for good or for ill, the success or failure of economic systems. Said differently, an economic system's success will be shown to be substantially dependent on its coherence with the demands of human biology, while incongruity with the demands of human biology will typically result in economic degradation and failure, such as was experienced by the former Soviet Union.

Classical economics calls this instinctive biological behavior enlightened self-interest. But there is nothing enlightened about the raw, aggressive selfishness that evolution demands. And, likewise, there is nothing enlightened about the same raw, aggressive selfishness, or greed, that the free market demands. Most of us don't like to think about it, but selfishness, whether disguised or blatant, compels all our actions and motivations.[3] Frequently we cloak it in socially acceptable language or concepts, but in the end, it is this instinctive compulsion that drives our behavior. So in this work, we will examine not just how this instinctive drive fits with the nature and precepts of capitalism and socialism but also how this instinctive drive can destroy such systems.

What we will be examining is the degree to which capitalism and socialism are compatible with genetic selfishness. However, it should be obvious, at least on the surface, that while capitalism, with its dependence

---

2 Pierre Teilhard de Chardin, *The Phenomenon of Man*, trans. Bernard Wall (New York: Harper Brothers Publishers, 1959), 218.

3 This notion is contrary to the typical introspective and therapeutic teachings of psychology and psychiatry. However, as we will see, the genetically imposed trait of selfishness, necessary for the preservation and evolution of the species, is uniform across all domains of life; and because of that simple fact, it must always take precedence over other motivational factors.

on competing factors of self-interest, is fully congruent with the basic human motivation of selfishness, socialism, on the other hand, with its abnegation of human selfishness, is indisputably incongruent. However, in practice, no system is pure. Neither capitalism nor socialism has ever been cleanly implemented, although the Soviet Union, from 1917 through the early 1990s; the Eastern European countries, from the mid-1950s through the early 1990s; and China, from the mid-1940s to the mid-1970s, have come very close. Close enough, in fact, that in combination with the United States as representative of capitalism, they form a workable base for analysis.

Fortunately, the data is adequate, or at least good enough, to allow for screening out the noise and yielding useable information. The hard part, however, is to determine to what extent capitalism or free enterprise elements can be incorporated into a socialist economy without severely diluting its benefits and then doing exactly the same thing for a capitalist economy by examining the degree to which socialist reforms can be introduced into a capitalist economy without diminishing its capacity for growth and wealth creation. My preliminary guess, based on considerations of biologically determined human motivations, is that capitalism can withstand considerable dilution without material erosion of its principal advantage of high economic growth and wealth creation; while, in contrast, socialism can tolerate very little dilution before its principal advantage of economic fairness is lost. I believe the historical data will demonstrate this.

Capitalism, while believed to be the greatest engine of economic growth and wealth creation ever devised by humankind, is subject to three self-destructive defects that are so problematic as to neutralize its benefits, causing the capitalist economy to be as unjust as the socialist economy and, if not corrected, resulting in collapse of the system and possibly even disintegration of civic order.

These defects, if left unchecked, are

1. the inevitability of extreme income and wealth inequality, producing momentum toward the breakdown of society;

2. the tendency toward the monopoly control of industry and the channels of distribution, finance, and resources, all of which eliminates the self-regulating advantage of a free enterprise system;

3. the despoliation of the natural environment.

Therefore, the final part of this work will be to explore alternatives, for the United States or any capitalist economy, to find the balance between economic growth and economic fairness. There are only a few economies in the world that have been able to simultaneously provide a fair distribution of wealth among its citizens and sustain a level of growth sufficient to provide for an expanding population. The best examples of these are the Nordic nations, Germany, France, and Austria.

It is my position that the solution lies in recognition of our biologically imposed imperative of selfishness and in its utilization to construct a better economy, all within the constraints of resource and environmental limits.

PART ONE

The Biological Imperative

There is no exception to the rule that every organic being naturally increases at so high a rate, that if not destroyed, the earth would soon be covered by the progeny of a single pair.
Charles Darwin, *The Origin of Species*

CHAPTER ONE

Evolution

I ASSUME THAT MOST people reading this book have a reasonably good working knowledge of the principles of evolution and natural selection, but just to establish a common understanding, this chapter is a summary of Charles Darwin's monumental theory, as modified by the Neo-Darwinian Synthesis, which brings in Mendelian heritability and the entire theory of genetics, neither one of which was known to Darwin at the time he developed his theories.

In 1859, Charles Darwin published a nearly five-hundred-page book that he labeled an abstract of his theory of biological evolution. The full title of his book was *On the Origin of Species by Means of Natural Selection, or the Preservation of Favoured Races in the Struggle for Life.* This is commonly shortened to *The Origin of Species*, but the full title, I believe, is a helpful reminder of Darwin's intent because he introduces his two key innovations: *natural selection* and *the struggle for life.*

The Struggle for Life

In *The Origin of Species* and in his earlier (1839) book *The Voyage of the Beagle*, Darwin observed and was deeply impressed by the quantity, variety, and complexity of life forms everywhere in the world. He also observed that all of life was involved in an unrelenting struggle for existence—animals against animals, animals against plants, animals against insects, insects against animals, insects against plants, and so forth. In addition to conflicts and competition with other life forms, he also saw that all of life struggled with environmental factors, like weather, windstorms, too much rain, too little rain, erosion, disease, and the whole multitude risk factors of nature.

In all this torrent of distress, he discerned a natural logic behind every story of unrelenting violence, death, famine, and destruction. Influenced by the work of Thomas Malthus, he began to see the necessary implication of this condition of natural warfare, because absent natural enemies or unfavorable environmental factors, populations would rapidly expand beyond the carrying capacity of the planet. Again, following Malthus, he came to understand that the evolution, growth, and survival of all organic being depended on the control of population that resulted from the competition among living organisms. Moreover, (as explained below) he also came to the realization that the diversity and sheer numbers within each species were necessary for long-term survival of the species. He stated this life-sustaining population equation thusly:

> There is no exception to the rule that every organic being naturally increases at so high a rate, that if not destroyed, the earth would soon be covered by the progeny of a single pair.[4]

So Darwin found that the struggle for existence, fueled by every organism's hardwired selfishness, was necessary for nature to maintain balance. But it was more than that. Uncontrolled or runaway population growth of all living things, which would result from an absence of deadly selfish competition, would quickly exhaust the planet's resources (and space), and all life, with the possible exception of its most primitive forms, would disappear from earth. Also, as a correlative to his notion of the necessity for the struggle for existence, he recognized that high rates of reproduction were logically necessary to assure a wide variety of genetic traits so that the essential process of natural selection could work.

---

4   Charles Darwin, *On the Origin of Species* ... (New York: The Penguin Group [USA] Inc., 2003), 63.

CHARLES L. LADNER

Natural Selection

Darwin's concept of natural selection was exceedingly simple, yet it comprised the hinge to the nineteenth century paradigm shift that moved the philosophical and theologically based understanding of life forward to the empirical, science-based understanding that undergirds the whole structure of modern biology and natural science.

In describing natural selection, Darwin reminds us that we should keep in mind that all living organisms are constantly under attack. For example, an animal may be threatened by larger animals that see it as food, it may be attacked by bloodsucking insects, it may be vulnerable to pathogens or disease-bearing organisms, and of course, it is subject to all the vagaries of climate and weather. At the same time, that very same animal may itself be attacking smaller animals and destroying vegetation for food while likely competing with other members of its own species, as well as creatures of other species, for access to the same food. Thus, in the context of the war in nature, it should be obvious that any small advantage that a creature may have in comparison to its peers means that over time, if its descendants inherit the advantage and pass it on to future generations, the group with the advantage will thrive, while those without the advantage will diminish. This is natural selection. The routine operations of nature will select the group or species that will continue.

Genetic variety is essential to the process, and it was believed that mutations are the source of most of the variety among living organisms. When an animal or any organism reproduces, there occasionally arise genetic errors called mutations. While some mutations could be harmful to the organism, most are benign. But from time to time, a mutation occurs that will give the offspring an advantage. It could be the ability to run faster so it can escape from predators, it could be greater strength so it can better fight off competitors or more easily capture victims, it could be a resistance to disease, or it could be superior eyesight so it can more readily find food. But whatever the advantage may be, it is likely that the organism will live better, longer, or more successfully than its peers with the advantage. It will be more fit. Thus, in time, over many generations, the group without the advantage will lose out in the fight for survival. It will diminish and possibly become extinct. It will be selected out.

Darwin's use of the term *natural selection* to describe this process has always been recognized as a poor choice of words, which even he himself acknowledged.[5] That's why it is often referred to as survival of the fittest. As for the inadequacy of the term *natural selection*, it can be first noted that the word *selection* implies an active predetermined activity, whereas what is really happening in natural selection is a passive random activity because mutations randomly occur without purpose. And second, it's not an activity involving selection, but rather it is an activity involving elimination. The less favored organism is eliminated. The more favored organism survives. Natural selection, in the words of Darwin, "acts solely through the preservation of variations in some way advantageous, which consequently endure."[6]

At the conclusion of the *Origin of Species*, Darwin wrapped up his theory in a beautiful, almost-poetic paragraph as follows:

> It is interesting to contemplate a tangled bank, clothed with many plants of many kinds, with birds singing on the bushes, with various insects flitting about, and with worms crawling through the damp earth, and to reflect that these elaborately constructed forms, so different from each other, and dependent upon each other in so complex a manner, have all been produced by laws acting around us. These laws, taken in the largest sense being, Growth with Reproduction; Variability from the indirect and direct action of the conditions of life, and from use and disuse: a Ratio of Increase as to lead to a Struggle for Life, and as a consequence to Natural Selection, entailing Divergence of Character and the Extinction of less improved forms.

---

5   Darwin, 61.

6   Darwin, 103.

CHARLES L. LADNER

Thus, from the War of Nature, from famine and death, the most exalted object which we are capable of conceiving, namely, the production of higher animals, directly follows. There is a grandeur in this view of life, with its several powers, having been originally breathed by the Creator into new forms or into one; and that, whilst this planet has gone cycling on according to the fixed law of gravity, from so simple a beginning endless forms most beautiful and most wonderful have been, and are being evolved.[7]

The Neo-Darwinian Synthesis

Darwin's theory, when first published, was greeted with great enthusiasm by all but the most fervent theist. Much of the Christian community saw Darwin's work as a denial of the Old Testament book of Genesis, preferring instead to place their trust in the notion of instantaneous creation by the Divine Creator rather than to interpret evolution as a divinely inspired process revealed by empirical science. Such groups, much reduced in size, still persist in the twenty-first century, over 160 years after the publication of *The Origin of Species*. But notwithstanding the absurdity of the creationists' passion, there also was legitimate scientific skepticism because Darwin left unanswered the whole question of exactly how inheritance worked. What were its biological mechanisms?

Up to the early twentieth century, the evolutionists appeared to have no answer. But in 1902, scientists in England, France, and Germany rediscovered the work of Gregor Mendel. Mendel was an Augustinian monk resident in an abbey in Brno, Moravia (now the Czech Republic). There, during the 1850s and '60s, he conducted detailed experiments using different varieties of pea plants, from which he was able to derive the rules of inheritance. He cultivated and tested approximately

---

7   Darwin, 507.

twenty-eight thousand plants. His work was published in 1865 in an obscure Moravian scientific journal and never came to the attention of the mainstream scientific community until 1902, eighteen years after his death and forty-three years after the initial publication of *The Origin of Species*. James Watson describes the work of this humble cleric as a tour de force:

> The experiments were brilliantly designed and painstakingly executed, and his analysis of the results was insightful and deft ... Unlike other biologists of that time, he approached the problem quantitatively. Rather than simply noting that crossbreeding of red and white flowers resulted in some red and some white offspring, Mendel actually counted them, realizing that the ratios of red to white progeny might be significant— as indeed they are.[8]

Mendel is now recognized as the "Father of Genetics" because prior to his discoveries, no one had the slightest idea how inheritance actually worked. Yet notwithstanding his findings, which detailed the provable and replicable rules of inheritance, it really wasn't until the 1960s that scientists were able to finally close the loop by identifying the physical carriers of heritable traits that make up the organism.

So despite Mendel's contribution, scientists in the early part of the twentieth century still could not fully answer the question, How does inheritance work? They recognized that some, yet to be identified, physical object within the embryonic cells carried the heritable characteristics. They called these mystery objects genes, but what they were, where they resided, how they acted, and how they contained, received, and transmitted the heritable factors took decades of exhaustive research by scientists throughout the world.

Curiously, during the nineteenth century, a good part of the necessary research, like Mendel's, had already been done, but the

---

8   James D. Watson, *DNA: The Story of the Genetic Revolution* (New York: Alfred A. Knopf, 2017), 8.

connections between Darwin's work and that of others had yet to be made. For example, in 1884, with improved optics, scientists discovered the existence of long stringy bodies within the nucleus of every living cell. They called them chromosomes, but they had no idea what function they carried out until in 1902, when a Columbia University medical student, Walter Sutton, realized that these strange bodies were the likely location of the genes that Mendel had originally described. Following Sutton's intuitive finding, Professor Thomas Hunt Morgan and his team, also at Columbia, over many years of painstaking experimentation using fruit flies (*Drosophila melanogaster*) as replicators, put together a complete and detailed portrayal of the genetic mechanism, which was published as *The Mechanism of Mendelian Heredity* in 1915. It still remains a definitive source. Now with Mendel's theory of heredity and Morgan's explication of its mechanics, Darwin's theory was reasonably complete.

Yet there still remained the nagging question of what exactly comprised a gene and where exactly within the chromosome was it located and how did it contain the plan or design of the phenotype's characteristics and what was the means for its transfer and actualization within the phenotype?

Evolution was proved and incontestably demonstrated to be correct. With the inclusion of the Mendelian genetic findings, the circle was closed. Little doubt remained among the scientific community and most of the general public as to its truth. But much more was to come. And that is the subject of the next chapter.

CHAPTER TWO

The Cell, DNA, Genes, and Selfish Behavior

The Similarity of Plants and Animals

ALL LIVING THINGS consist of cells or cellular matter. Among the universe of living things, there is extraordinary diversity ranging from single-cell organisms, like prokaryotes (bacteria), to multicelled organisms, like fungi, sponges, trees, lettuce, fish, insects, mammals, and people.

However, we living things are unique, not only in our makeup of cells but also remarkably, considering the vast differences in the kingdom of living things, no matter whether we are plants or animals, we all are made up of cells that are eerily similar. There is not much difference between a lettuce cell and a mosquito cell, and there is not much difference between a mosquito cell and a human cell.

The diagram shown below illustrates the similarities between a plant and an animal cell. In carefully examining this diagram, it is evident that in terms of components, both are very similar. They both have the same parts: nucleus, DNA, ribosomes, mitochondria, cytoplasm, Golgi apparatus, etc. And for the most part, they carry out the same functions of survival and reproduction. They generate the means for their survival by manufacturing proteins that serve to replace worn-out parts and also serve as the fundamental building blocks of cellular growth. And they reproduce or replicate themselves mainly by means of cell division. In addition, they perform all the ordinary functions necessary to sustain existence. They mobilize and circulate energy inputs, dispose of waste, and through their DNA, provide the directions and control functions governing the continuous life of the cell.

Figure 1. Plant versus Animal Cell

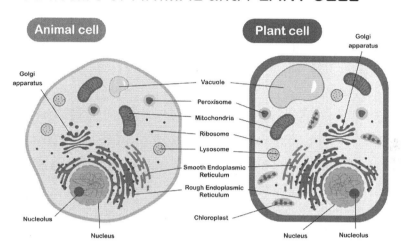

Biology diagram ● ● ●

Structure of ANIMAL and PLANT CELL

However, as we all know, there are significant differences. Plants, for example, require carbon dioxide for life and expel oxygen as waste, while animals do just the opposite. They take in oxygen to convert to useable energy and expel carbon dioxide as waste. What's interesting in all this is that many of the same parts are involved in these disparate processes performing vastly different functions, made possible by directions encoded within the plant and animal genes. As an example, consider the mitochondria, of which there may be hundreds or even thousands in a single cell. In both animals and plants, the mitochondria produce ATP (adenosine triphosphate), which is the primary source of cellular energy, except the animal's mitochondria uses oxygen in the process, while the plant's mitochondria uses the products of photosynthesis.

There are other differences. One of these relates to the outward structure of the cell. The plant cell has a rigid wall formed from cellulose, while the animal cell wall is flexible and supple. Another difference is that the plant cell contains a saclike feature called the vacuole, which is mostly filled with water providing a reserve for plant sustenance while, at the same time, providing a measure of rigidity to the cell. (Remember, in contrast to most animals, plants have no skeletal structure, so they need the rigid cell walls and internal vacuoles to provide support and definition of form.)

Quite apart from these differences, the important thing to keep in mind is the extraordinary similarity between plant and animal cells and especially the fact that both have a nucleus within that there are chromosomes, DNA, and genes. And from this, one can readily draw the inference that plants, just like animals, are possessed of the same relentless need to survive and reproduce. They, too, are selfish.

Chromosomes, DNA, and Genes: The Seat of Selfish Behavior?

So now we come to the point where we must discuss where this selfishness—this drive for survival and reproduction—originates. What is the source? Where is the seat of selfishness?

A few pages back, we left the story of how the theory of evolution developed with the discovery of chromosomes and the progress made by Thomas Hunt Morgan in assigning the location of the genes to the chromosomes. But what exactly are genes? How do they work? How do they learn, record, and transport information? What do they look like? All this was a big mystery.

In 1869, well before the rediscovery of Mendel, the work of Morgan, and the formulation of the modern synthesis, a Swiss biochemist, Friedrich Miescher, discovered DNA (deoxyribonucleic acid). But neither he nor anyone else at that time assigned any importance to it even though it was located within the cellular nucleus in or on the chromosomes. Meanwhile, following Hunt's pioneering work, scientists throughout the world continued an ever more intense search for the nature of genes. Finally, in 1944, Oswald Avery and his colleagues at the Rockefeller Institute in New York published the results of their research that demonstrated that genes, the transforming principle that was the target of all this scientific effort, were associated with DNA. This was a bit of a shock. Scientists had earlier determined that the means by which genes stored and transmitted information was through some sort of code, and DNA, with only four base chemicals, was not a good candidate. Now with it having been demonstrated that the mysterious DNA molecule really was the locus of the gene, the competition among scientists really heated up, especially the competition between the American and British scientific establishments; so it was pure serendipity that when the breakthrough occurred, it was achieved by the partnership of James Watson (American) and Francis Crick (British), working at the Cavendish Laboratory in Cambridge.

The problem everyone was trying to solve was to determine the structure and functions of DNA with the expectation that it would reveal the secrets of the gene.

Along with all other researchers, Watson and Crick followed the standard experimental protocols; but when they, like others, made no meaningful progress, they began to think about the three-dimensional characteristics of the molecule, first concluding that it was shaped in the form of a helix.[9] To better visualize the object, they built physical models that looked like they were made out of Tinkertoys. They probably were not aware at the time that this simple technique was a true heuristic breakthrough. They found that the molecule was like a ladder with the frame or backbone made up of phosphate and the rungs made up of four chemicals: adenine, thymine, cytosine, and guanine, often abbreviated as ATCG.

Watson and Crick's breakthrough occurred in 1954. Since then, biology, genetics, biochemistry, molecular biology, and all other affiliated branches of the life sciences have advanced well beyond the wildest imagination of the early pioneers of this new field of study. Take for example the DNA molecule—we now know that it contains three billion base pairs, and if stretched out, it would measure about six feet from end to end.

---

9   A helix is a three-dimensional shape in the form of a corkscrew or spiral staircase.

Yet in each of our eleven trillion somatic cells, there is a nucleus containing twenty-three pairs of chromosomes in which there resides the DNA molecule. In other words, each one of us will have eleven trillion double-helix DNA molecules in our body.[10]

Genes, we have learned, are composed of many base pairs distributed along a strand of DNA. There are approximately twenty-three thousand potential combinations from which genes can be made. DNA is the physical substrate for genes. Genes represent the plan or schematic for the phenotype (organism). The instructions are implemented through the cellular production of proteins that are either retained within the cell for its own use or transferred out of the cell for the organism's use. In either case, the genetic instructions are embedded within the protein for expression at the level of the phenotype. It is this expression that constitutes the subject of natural selection. And that closes the circle. The organism that is selected, or not eliminated, is favored because its genetic expression makes it somehow better adapted than its peers. It does not tell us where the genes carrying the instinct for survival and reproduction reside within the DNA. Most likely, because these traits were historically the original needs without which the organism or phenotype could never have existed, one can infer that, like many other basic genotypic expressions, the drive for selfishness is scattered throughout most (possibly all) genetic loci.

The Search for the Origin of Selfish Behavior

In the foregoing chapters, with an eye on human behavior, the conversation is directed toward understanding the embedded instinct for survival and reproduction. This is done mainly by reference to Darwin's unchallenged assertion that while all other instincts, whether they be in plants or animals, may be necessary for their comfortable existence, it is exclusively the selfish instinct for survival and reproduction that

---

10   The exact count of cells in the human body is still an open question. The most recent estimate is 37.2 trillion cells, of which approximately twenty trillion are red blood cells, which have no nucleus or DNA.

not only enables natural selection—without which animate life itself couldn't have come into being—but also serves to activate all human behavior. And then following on this discussion, in logical progression, I asked the question, Where or how does this instinct originate? And how does it achieve physical actualization in the organism's body and mind? I do not think I have yet adequately answered this question, but in response, I would hope that the science describing the operations of the cell, DNA, and genes would begin to shed some light on the matter. Certainly, it does nothing to diminish Darwin's extraordinary insight that selfishness is the unconditional biological root of human behavior. But have I done enough? Maybe to feel fully confident in the proposition, we should dig deeper and see if we can find some indications of selfishness at the very edge of life.

It is standard evolutionary theory that the first sign of life on this planet arose in the form of prokaryotes (bacteria) and their near cousin archaea (of which little is known). Prokaryotes are unquestionably the most successful form of life ever to appear on earth. They are minute single-cell entities with genetic material in their chromosomes and DNA, ribosomes to synthesize proteins but have no encapsulated nucleus. They are ubiquitous; a single teaspoon of garden soil may contain upward of one billion prokaryotic cells.

There are an estimated thirty-seven trillion prokaryotes (bacteria) in or on every human body. No one has ever been able to determine their population, much less the number of species. Early in the planet's life, it is thought that prokaryotes first appeared 3.8 billion years ago, about 750 million years after the planet was formed. The early atmosphere contained little or no free oxygen, being mainly composed of carbon dioxide, nitrogen, carbon monoxide, and hydrogen sulfide. Yet prokaryotes emerged, thrived, and evolved, originally deriving their energy from what was available in the atmosphere and, later, by photosynthesis from the sun. It was the evolved ability to use hydrogen sulfide in the conversion of carbon dioxide that enabled the prokaryotes to derive energy from the sun by the process of photosynthesis. The critical byproduct of this process was to liberate free oxygen. And here is the important part: over the billions of years since prokaryote first employed photosynthesis, they created and continue to maintain the oxygen-rich atmosphere in which we and virtually all other living things live. Moreover, their other essential function is to ingest organic material and exhale more oxygen. Absent prokaryotes, our digestive systems would not function and no dead organic matter would ever decompose. It is not an overstatement to say that without prokaryotes, no life, including humans, could have ever come into existence on earth.

What is important is to know that even the first and most primitive evidence of life could not have appeared, thrived, and evolved without an inherent drive for survival and reproduction. Keeping in mind that life, in the form of prokaryotes, somehow emerged from a soup of raw, lifeless chemicals, the fundamental instinct of selfishness should thus be understood as the essential quality that differentiates life from nonlife.

The Elusive Mystery of Scale

When we think about things like cells, chromosomes, genes, DNA, and the like, it is easy to lose sight of the minute scale of what we are discussing. All the cellular and genetic actions and mechanics occur within the DNA molecule, which itself is contained inside the unimaginably small nucleus within the cell. To visualize the scale, consider this: it has been estimated that there about seventy-five trillion (75,000,000,000,000) cells in or about the human body. Half are prokaryotes or bacteria. They reside mostly in the intestinal tract, but they also are found in great quantity on the skin and the plaque on one's teeth. Bacteria are very small. A teaspoon of garden soil can contain anywhere from one hundred million to one billion individual bacteria cells. Moreover, these tiny single-cell organisms have many of the components of a human somatic cell; for example, they have ribosomes for protein production and anywhere from five hundred to 7,500 genes crammed into their DNA, located on or in circular chromosomes. In addition, here are two other examples of enormous genetic functionality packed into an unimaginably small prokaryotic space: *E. coli* has four thousand genes and *Haemophilius influenzae* DNA has 1.8 million base pairs yielding 1,757 genes.[11] These kind of things are not unusual. The microbial world is rife with scale anomalies. Nematodes, a worm comprising only 959 cells, has twenty thousand genes, compared with a human's twenty-three thousand; and while human DNA is composed of 3.5 million base pairs, the DNA of the lowly fern is composed of 160 million base pairs.[12]

Then when we come to the human, notwithstanding the bacterial cells that support human life, there are another thirty-seven trillion human cells, of which about twenty-six trillion are red blood cells that have no nucleus and no genetic functions but support the remaining eleven trillion cells that we normally think of as human somatic[13] cells (and that that has been the subject of the last several paragraphs). They, too, are very small; for example, there about one billion somatic cells in an average human finger.

So when we are talking about locating the genes within the DNA molecule, we are hoping for the near impossible. Yet in 2003, the Human Genome Project was completed, three years ahead of its fifteen-year schedule. This project, comparable in many ways to the WWII Manhattan project, mapped out and determined the exact location of each of the human genome's 3.5 billion base pairs within the DNA molecule. Looking to the future, this is the raw data needed for the science of genetics to fulfill the promise so abundantly prefigured by the work of Charles Darwin and Gregor Mendel.

Thus far, our process has been to first establish the scientifically given truth that biologically induced selfishness is dominant over all other human motivation. Then letting the science be our guide and following where it leads—beginning with the cell and its component parts, its functions, and its control mechanism—while then delving into the machinery of the genome and the behavioral patterns of genes residing within the DNA molecules, we have surveyed activity at the

---

11 Watson, 239.

12 Watson, 233, 236.

13 The term *somatic* refers to any cell other than a germ cell that takes part in the formation of the body, becoming differentiated into the various tissues, organs, etc.

genetic level, which, in the eyes of some researchers, gives the appearance of selfishness, almost as if individual genes possessed a consciousness and a capacity for thought. This, of course, is questionable, yet the behavior of genes themselves has engendered considerable controversy, which has us entering into the discussion of the question of whether an organism's need for self-preservation and reproduction has its seat at the level of the gene or has its origin in the genetic expression at the level of the organism.

Always in the background and serving as a first principle is the fact of evolution and natural selection. Absent this foundation, nothing in this book makes sense. The coherence and the integrity of this study is entirely dependent on what most informed people now view as the self-evident theory of evolution. Not only does it explain the development of living things over time but it also comes very close to explaining the origin of life itself. And the key that makes evolution work is the universal characteristic of all life that demands the biological imperatives of self-preservation and reproduction. And because all of life is implicated in this matter, we must begin with the smallest unit, the cell and its DNA.

The operations of an organism's cells and, within the cell, the instincts and preprogrammed behaviors encoded in its DNA represent the critical means by which the evolutionary determinism of a human being and, for that matter, the evolutionary determinism of all living things is carried out. Evolution is a fact. It applies to all living organisms—from the single-cell bacterium in our gut to the grass in our backyards, the mosquitos in the marsh, the elephants on the Savannah, and the humans all over the world. Everything living exists in a state of evolutionary flux. No living things are static. They all are imperceptibly adapting and changing all the time. Evolution is, thus, the fundamental condition of life.

As it affects living organisms, evolution proceeds in very small incremental steps. For most species, the length of the reproductive cycle combined with random nature of mutations and, thus, the enormous number of unsuccessful outcomes means that evolutionary change in larger organisms can take thousands of generations and tens of thousands of years. However, for tiny organisms—like the fruit fly or bacterium—where the reproductive cycle is short, change can occur in a matter of years. As an interesting illustration, here is an example from everyday life where evolutionary change is occurring right before our very eyes. In my view, this is a living laboratory that proves the truth of evolution.

First, we should recall that the term *evolution* describes the process carried out by a species adapting itself to either overcome an adverse environment (the physical environment or threatening organisms) or to improve itself to take advantage of an otherwise benign environment. The adapting organism will live, thrive, and reproduce; while the organism that does not adapt will die and not reproduce. Its line will terminate. This is called natural selection. Second, evolution is a trial and error process requiring millions of experiments in the form of reproduction and mutation, so if the reproductive cycle is very lengthy—as it is for large mammals (say, ten to twenty years)—then whatever adaptations are called for will occur in imperceptible increments over a very long time. On the other hand, for microscopically minute organisms, like bacteria, the reproductive cycle may be as short as fifteen minutes; thus millions and millions of trial and error experiments are done in only a few months. And in fact, we have actually seen this adaptation occur in real time in our own lives. In the space of only a few years, toxic bacteria that we once thought were eliminated by antibacterial pharmaceuticals have, through the process of natural selection, adapted and responded—as the *MRSA*, "superbugs"—resistant to the drugs that threatened to kill them off.[14] This is a perfect example of evolution in action. So one might ask, What causes an organism or, more properly, its genes and phenotype to react to threats, if only unconsciously, through the reproductive process? Well, as we have emphasized to the point of annoying redundancy, biologists long ago found that every living thing has its primary, overriding, and intractable mode of behavior

---

14   It is understood the mechanics involve either mutations, as in most cases of adaptation, or a process of horizontal transfer of genetic material unique to bacteria (prokaryotes).

predetermined by two persistent motivations to which all other actions are always subordinate: (1) self-preservation and (2) reproduction. Nothing else matters. Nothing. Summarized and said differently, we have called this essential quality of life biological selfishness. It applies as much to humans as it does to bacteria. Our actions are all subject to selfish determinism.

Accordingly, my goal is to use this knowledge to understand how biology determines economic behavior insofar as such behavior is embodied and expressed by the principal economic regimes that have competed with each for legitimacy since the time of Adam Smith and Karl Marx.

CHAPTER THREE

Socialization

The First Derivative of Selfishness

Thus far, the entire conversation in this book has been one of monotonous redundancy; as over and over again, I have narrowed the focus of human behavior to the need for survival and reproduction, which I shorthand as selfishness. So while grateful for the reader's forbearance and without in any way denying the primacy of selfishness as the fundamental engine of human behavior, I think now is the time to acknowledge another instinct rare in organisms other than humans but characteristically and uniformly common within all humans—an instinct that seems as powerful in determining the outcomes of life as the instinct for selfishness. And that is the genetically embedded proclivity for association with other humans—a need that is almost as fiercely compulsive as the drive for survival and reproduction.

Apart from prokaryotes, human beings are the most successful organisms on earth. There are nearly 7.5 billion of us. We adapt and live everywhere, in all climate zones. We build tools to extend our capacity for survival. We develop medical sciences to enhance the quality and duration of our lives. We develop extraordinarily strong and complex social, economic, and political structures for mutual protection and benefit. We do all this with our large and efficient brain, an organ that no other life form has or even comes close to having.

In the struggle for existence, humans have absolutely no physical advantage. We are helpless. We have less strength, we cannot outrun, and we cannot outfight our natural predators. We are susceptible to disease-bearing pathogens, and in our natural state, we can exist only within a very narrow range of temperature before we succumb to hypothermia or heat exhaustion. In a natural state, survival over the cold winter months is a matter of pure chance. And apart from vegetative matter, there is virtually no other source of food available to us.

Yet notwithstanding our inbred inadequacies, we have flourished and triumphed over all of nature. Why? The answer is obvious. Unlike every other living creature, we humans have evolved a powerful brain that has enabled us to modify our environment and make tools, protective clothing, shelter, and fire while at the same time developing all the other physical instruments that allow us to neutralize our weaknesses, subdue our enemies, and dominate the natural world

But assuredly among primitive humans, the most consequential product of our emerging intellect was not so much our fabrication of material things as it was the evolution of the capacity for communication and cooperation, which permitted the pooling of capabilities, knowledge, and resources that provided the means for survival. Absent the evolution of the intellect, we would still be members of an inconspicuous species living in trees and just barely hanging on to life in a competitively cruel and vicious world. It would take the evolution of cooperative social structures in the form of extended families, tribes, or small communities to liberate humans from their inherent limitations. In short, our cognitive capacity and our propensity for socialization, both of which are the product of natural selection, are the instruments of adaptation that secure our biological success.

Many evolutionary biologists believe that the origin of emergent human social organization can be found in an initial pattern of eusocial behavior thought to be common among early hominids. Eusociality of a group entails the practice of reproductive division of labor and cooperative care of the young, reinforced by overlapping generations. The eminent evolutionary biologist E. O. Wilson sees this primitive social structure as providing a sufficient division of labor to allow the group to thrive, with some group members devoting their entire life to reproduction and raising the young, while the remaining group members being fully involved in hunting and gathering food for the group as a whole. Wilson and others perceive this structure as biological

CHARLES L. LADNER

in origin and analogous to the social organization of ants, termites, or bees. However, unlike ants and bees, human eusociality could have been only a gateway, a way station, toward the development of highly non-eusocial complex societies made possible by the continued evolution of intellectual capacity for memory and innovation and self-awareness.[15]

That there exists in humans a powerful drive for socialization is questioned by no one. However, the derivation of this instinct is not settled science and revolves around disagreements as to the unit of selection. Is it the organism as a whole, is it the genes, or is it both—that is to say, is it multilevel? The current consensus appears to be that it is multilevel. Darwin himself even raised this possibility.

In analyzing the operation of the instinct for socialization, Wilson identifies two initial idiosyncratic traits:[16]

- "The intense, even obsessive interest of people in other people ... Research psychologists have found that all normal humans are geniuses at reading the intentions of others, whereby they evaluate, proselytize, bond, cooperate, gossip, and control."
- "A second diagnostic hereditary trait of human behavior is the overpowering instinctual urge to belong to groups ... A person's membership in his group—his tribe—is a large part of his identity."

These building blocks of social behavior began to emerge perhaps one million years ago as prehumans in Africa joined together for self-preservation and reproduction. The human mind was still evolving, and the tendencies toward group dynamics were evolving with it. Mental,

---

15   Edward O. Wilson, *The Meaning of Human Existence* (New York: W. W. Norton & Company, 2014), 3–34.

Edward O. Wilson, *The Social Conquest of the Earth* (New York: W. W. Norton & Company, 2012).

Martin A. Nowak, Corine E. Tarnita, and Edward O. Wilson, *The Evolution of Eusociality*, Nature, 2010 August 26; 466:1,057–1,062.

Herbert Gintis, review of *The Social Conquest of the Earth*, by Edward O. Wilson, *BioScience* 62, no. 11 (November 2012): 987–991.

16   Wilson (2014), 30–31.

emotional, and instinctive acuity continued to grow. But it must always be remembered that the brain evolved solely as an instrument of survival, and so the evolution of the instinct for social behavior evolved as an instrument of survival too.

Nevertheless, in the operation of social and political structures, there is persistent and enduring conflict between the selfish instincts of individuals (a product of individual selection) and the cooperative needs of the group selection (a product of group selection). Quoting Wilson again,

> So it came to pass that humans are forever conflicted ... They are suspended in unstable and constantly changing positions between two extreme forces that created us. We are unlikely to yield completely to either force as the ideal solution to our social and political turmoil. To give in completely to the instinctual urgings born from individual selection would be to dissolve society. At the opposite extreme, to surrender to the urgings from group selection would turn us into angelic robots—the outsized equivalents of ants.[17]

Everything that follows in this book regarding economic systems, which are really specialized social structures, is entirely a function of the fundamental biological conflict so aptly described by Edward Wilson.

So in the following chapters, while much of the analysis is based on the unit of selection at the level of the genes (which finds expression at the level of the organism), because this best explains the behavioral characteristics of people living within and subject to both socialist and capitalist systems and thus aids in understanding the historic fragility or durability of each, it is not the whole story. For if adaptation to changing circumstances is the product of natural selection, then there is no reason why such adaptation cannot be expressed at a group or societal level.

---

17 Wilson (2014), 33.

CHARLES L. LADNER

I am convinced that it is, and for that reason, this phenomenon is discussed in chapter 13 when all the loose strands are brought together. I hope it will be seen as a comprehensive account.

* * *

Well, so much for the biology (for now anyway).

To recap, in the introduction, I discussed the drive for survival and reproduction, which dominates the instinctual constitution of all living things. Then in the next two chapters, I demonstrated that without this powerful, deeply rooted, all-enveloping instinct for survival and reproduction, which I call selfishness, life itself would have failed to evolve. Finally, I discussed the opposite instinct that directs humanity to socialization, which emerged in humans as the principal and essential means enabling human survival and reproduction.

I now move to the realm of economics, where I will attempt to unpack the doctrines of socialism and capitalism. This should allow us to propose a hypothesis regarding the suitability of each of these two systems to the human need or compulsion for genetic fitness, which then will first be tested by reference to actual real-life historical experience and, second, will be used to form the foundation of policy proposals or, perhaps better said, policy ideas for application in the United States and other nations.

PART TWO

The Economic Systems

When you can measure what you are speaking about, and express it in numbers, you know something about it; but when you cannot measure it, when you cannot express it in numbers, your knowledge is of a meagre and unsatisfactory kind.

Lord Kelvin, *Lecture on Electrical Units of Measurement.* May 3,1883

CHAPTER FOUR

Setting the Scene

IT WOULD SEEM that in a broad historical sense, the provenance of all economic systems can be seen as falling into one of two mutually exclusive categories:

- The first is what I will call an *organic model,* where the participants are largely free to do as they wish. They can be at great personal risk, but they have no limits on their economic freedom other than those placed on them by nature. An organic system can be visualized as being synonymous with the philosophical state of nature.
- The second economic model is what I will call an *authoritarian system.* This is a hierarchical mode of organizing society and its economic expression in which most participants are subject to discipline and coercive regimentation. It is typically identified with political control of the economy by a single individual or a small group.

This division of economic systems is proposed as the progenitor of the two modern economic systems we will be studying. The *organic* model I would suggest is the source from which the later free enterprise system is derived. Likewise, the *authoritarian* model may be seen as an antecedent of today's socialism. At the very primitive level of early human existence, which we will be discussing in this chapter, the distinction between the two systems is the degree to which the system itself imposes limitations on the individual's freedom of economic action.

The *organic* model is not properly a system but rather the continuous operation of a group in its rational response to external threats. It is a description of what was developed by *Homo sapiens* as the earliest form of human economic behavior, namely the economy of the family, extended family, or tribe. In a sense, it may be seen as the first organized culture in which there is a primitive division of labor and a protohierarchical leadership structure.

Preceded by an estimated six million years of evolutionary hominid development, *Homo sapiens* (modern humans) appeared about three hundred thousand years ago in Africa. Living like animals in the wild, *Homo sapiens*, like his hominid ancestors, was migratory or nomadic in nature, operating in small groups in search of food, whose life was entirely centered on survival and reproduction.[18] In the words of Thomas Hobbes, it was an existence that was "nasty, brutish and short."

In one manner or another, the *organic* economic model was that that nourished *Homo sapiens* until the advent of organized communal living, which began to appear perhaps twenty-five thousand years ago. Thus, for almost the entire extent of human life on earth (275,000 years), the *organic* model was its primary mode of economic existence. However, after the long duration of this torture, a new model first began to flicker and slowly emerge. This was the settled nonmigratory community contained within permanent or semipermanent encampments. Such groupings were slow to develop, and it was about fifteen thousand years before anything resembling a town or village began to crop up. Jericho, thought to be the first town, was settled by 8,000 BCE, and various settlements in Egypt are dated from 6,000 BCE, while the Mesopotamian/Sumerian network of cities, often called the cradle of civilization, date from about 5,000 BCE.

Historian Chester Starr points out that with the very first permanent settlements, class distinctions "evolved rather quickly."[19] These nascent societies, almost of necessity, evolved such that in the course of time,

---

18   G. J. Sawyer, Viktor Deak, and Esteban Sarmiento, *The Last Human: A Guide to Twenty-Two Species of Extinct Humans* (New Haven: Yale University Press, 2007).
19   Chester A. Starr, *A History of the Ancient World* (New York: Oxford University Press, 1991), 42.

they would become characterized by the following traits: "the presence of firmly organized states which had definite boundaries and systematic political institutions, under political and religious leaders who directed and also maintained society; the distinction of social classes; the economic specialization of men as farmers, trader, or artisan, each dependent upon his fellows; and the conscious development of the arts and intellectual attitudes."[20] Moreover, we know from documented history that with the advent of civilization in the form of organized states and cities, the prevailing *organic* economic system gave way to a more coercive means of organizing the economy in the form of *authoritarian* systems. And it could not be otherwise, for discipline and the loss of personal freedom were the only possible ways that the safety, security, comfort, and leisure afforded by civilization could, at that early stage, be secured. Later, much more complex societies would develop that provided all the benefits of civilization without demanding the total sacrifice of personal liberties (e.g., Athens and Rome).

The Influence of Genetic Instincts on the Economic Behavior of Early Humans

The next two sections of this chapter will examine the economies of Egypt and Rome. Both are near-perfect examples of the division of economic systems into the *organic* and *authoritarian* categories. In both cases, while there was substantial variability in their respective political conditions, each of their economies endured, mostly unchanged for a

---

20   Starr (1991), 27.

considerable length of time and generally little affected by the political winds of the day.[21]

The ancient Egyptian economy took shape as an *authoritarian* system early in the First Dynasty (i.e., 3050–2686 BCE). As an economic system, it was highly successful and did not unravel until after the Muslim conquest of Egypt in 641 CE. The Egyptian *authoritarian* economic model lasted, substantially unchanged, for about three thousand to 3,600 years. In contrast, the Roman system, which may be seen as a natural outgrowth of the Neolithic *organic* model, was—for all intents and purposes—a capitalist or free enterprise system. Rome was supposedly founded in 753 BCE, and it died with the Muslim conquest of Constantinople in 1453 CE, having prevailed for approximately two thousand years.

My analysis of economic systems is grounded on the two fundamental genetic predispositions that affect human behavior: selfishness and socialization. In any society, these dispositions are, of course, always present and always determinative of economic outcomes; but typically, one will prevail over the other in giving shape to society and to its economic expression. In the case of ancient Egypt, the initial drive toward socialization was the predominate organizing principle of the economy, although, very quickly among the elites, their self-interests were subject to little restraint, and what started out as voluntary movement toward association with others for mutual economic gain

---

21 Egypt's political/religious autocracy lasted for approximately three thousand years; however, it was broken up by three periods of political revolt and instability. They were (1) the first intermediate period, 2181–1991 BCE, 190 years; (2) the second intermediate period, 1674–1549 BCE, 125 years; and (3) the third intermediate period, 1069–653 BCE, 416 years. An interesting study of the inundation during the Ptolemaic period (305–30 BCE) recently published in the journal *Nature Communications* suggests that volcanic activity throughout the world affected the African monsoons such that they were reduced in volume. This, in turn, resulted in much reduced Egyptian inundations, which resulted in widespread famine, leading to socioeconomic instability and the fall of the prevailing political order (J. G. Manning, "Volcanic Suppression of Nile Summer Flooding Triggers Revolt and Constrains Interstate Conflict in Ancient Egypt," *Nature Communications*, DOI 10.1038/s41467-17-00957-y.

rapidly coalesced on the elites who seized and consolidated the bulk of the economic benefits for themselves, leaving little more than subsistence income for the mass of people. And while it is true that from time to time self-interests erupted in revolts or civic disorder among the general population, such events were mostly in response to societal breakdowns from famine or wars.

Nevertheless, no matter what the state of political instability, the economic system continued to function in the background and was quite likely sufficient to have been instrumental in the restoration of political order after periods of distress. On the other hand, as we will see, in the case of Rome, once the drive for socialization successfully created the republic, the sublimated instinct for survival and reproduction rapidly, and perhaps simultaneously, arose among the people to dominate the structure of the resultant civilization. The expression of this selfish behavior found its form in the private ownership of property and the free trade that characterized Rome's economy and fueled its political hegemony.

The Egyptian Model

To illustrate how remarkably effective was the thrust of civilization and how rapidly humans moved from the chaos of their *organic* economy to an organized and almost modern way of life, albeit under the mantle of coercive discipline in an *authoritarian* system, the following discussion of the early economy of Egypt might be helpful.

The single most important fact regarding the ancient economy of Egypt is the Nile River. The Nile is the longest river in the world, flowing south to north 4,132 miles from its origin in Central Africa to the Mediterranean Sea. It drains approximately 1.3 million square miles, some 10% of the total African landmass. In Egypt, it runs about 850 miles. The southern part, which is barely navigable, flows for 150 miles through or over a series of six cataracts surrounded by rocky barren land. Then continuing from south to north, from the final cataract, northward to Memphis (about fifteen miles south of present-day Cairo), the river runs for five hundred miles through a valley of arable land ten to fifteen miles wide, bordered on either side by deserts and mountains. Finally, from Cairo to the sea, it flows another 150 miles through the Delta, which is shaped like an equilateral triangle, narrow at the base and widening to 156 miles at its terminus where it descends into the Mediterranean. The land of the Nile valley and the Delta is exceedingly fertile, but there is little rainfall, so absent the annual flooding, which is called the inundation, it is virtually useless as a base for agronomy.

The annual inundation made all the difference. The inundation was the signal event each year. The river began rising in early July and could remain at flood stage for as much as one hundred days before it began to recede. The waters not only irrigated the parched land but they also deposited tons of rich organic silt from the hinterlands of Africa. The flood contained an enormous quantity of water that drained and concentrated along the Nile valley and the riverine delta, almost the entire product of the winter monsoons from the breadth of equatorial Africa.

In the fifth century BC, the Greek historian Herodotus visited Egypt and had this to say regarding the flooded landscape: "When the Nile overflows, the whole country is converted into a sea, and the towns, which alone remain above water, look like islands in the Aegean."[22] There is no better description of Egypt during the season of the inundation than this.

However, notwithstanding the benefit of the inundation to the fields and lands on the immediate borders of the river and streams in the Delta, most of its potential value was lost without management of this extraordinary hydraulic asset. What was needed and was put in place was an extensive network of transmission and distribution canals, holding basins, sluice gates, and all the other infrastructure of an effective water management system to maximize the distribution of the inundation to all possible arable land.

---

22 Herodotus, *The Histories Book 2*, trans. Aubrey De Selincourt (Baltimore: Penguin Books, Inc., 1955), 97, 137.

About 5000 BCE, small tribal villages were scattered throughout the Nile valley and Delta. But by 3000 BC, the villages in the lower Nile and the Delta had coalesced into a kingdom; and shortly thereafter, the villages in the upper Nile came under their control. Now with a unified kingdom, (the Old Kingdom, 2686–2181), the kings and the temple priests began the process of organizing the economy.

The capital was located at Memphis. In the history of Egypt, this was a fateful event to establish a city that would centralize the administrative and religious life of the kingdom. "Towns are like electric transformers," said Fernand Braudel. "They increase tension, accelerate the rhythm of exchange and constantly recharge human life. They were born of the oldest and most revolutionary division of labor: between work in the fields on the one hand and activities described as urban on the other … Towns generate expansion and are themselves generated by it. But even when towns do not create growth, they undoubtedly channel its course to their own advantage."[23]

Braudel well described what almost certainly happened with the centralization at Memphis. The land fell under the control of the king, the elites, and the temples. The agricultural bounty was vastly improved by the development of a sophisticated water management system, which supported not only the lavish lifestyles of the kings and the elites but also the construction of massive temples and monuments. The pyramids and the Great Sphinx at Memphis date from this period. But as Braudel predicted, the city and central government did, in fact, take control of the agricultural wealth and "channel its course to their own advantage." Moreover, the people lost not just the economic benefits of the land but also the value of their personal labor, as they were required to work the land, build and maintain the irrigation systems, and contribute their labor in the construction of the temples, pyramids, and great monuments.

Thus, Egypt became the epitome and perfect example of an *authoritarian* economic system. It was a cruel and oppressive system.

---

23   Fernand Braudel, *The Structures of Everyday Life Volume I*, trans. Sian Reynolds (New York: Harper & Row Publishers Inc., 1981), 479.

Probably less than 10% of the population benefited, while the rest lived in a subsistence mode of gross servitude. Yet considered as a national economy, Egypt was the wealthiest and most successful economy in the ancient world. It endured for three thousand years.[24]

The Roman Model

From its outset, the Roman state was constructed on the foundation of a capitalist free enterprise economy—the type of economic system that was not to be seen in the west for more than a thousand years after the fall of the Western Empire in 476 CE. To be sure, the Eastern Empire (Byzantium) continued until 1453, but it hardly embraced capitalism with the same enthusiasm as the Western Empire. This was mainly due to the penetration of religious ideals and a focus on the hereafter into everyday life, along with the growing political influence of the monks and clergy, the empire's loss of rural provinces as a source of military manpower, and the concurrent reduction in the geographic scope of its foreign markets.

In embracing the capitalist / free enterprise model, Rome adopted a form of social organization that was the polar opposite of the Egyptian

---

24 During the last third of this three-thousand-year period, while in the villages and farming estates of rural Egypt, which represented all but a small portion of the land and population, the *authoritarian* model prevailed and poverty characterized the countryside, among the elites and leadership, the situation changed radically. In 332 BCE, Alexander the Great took control of Egypt and its population of three to four million. At the same time, he began the construction of his new city of Alexandria. This was a Greek city poised on the banks of the Mediterranean, just east of the Delta. It grew to a population of about four hundred thousand and was entirely oriented to the exploitation of Egypt's natural resources, servile population, and wealth. Most critically, it introduced a free enterprise economy into Egypt. Alexandria was a planned city, the largest, wealthiest, and most beautiful and culturally advanced city during the Hellenistic period (300 BCE–32 BCE). But in 32 BCE, the Greek-dominated state of Egypt fell to Rome, who then ruled Egypt until its conquest by the Muslims in 641 CE. During the Roman period, the *authoritarian* system began to break down because of Rome's encouragement of private property and free trade.

system. In Egypt, the state owned or controlled the means of production (farms and estates). In Rome, private citizens owned the means of production. In Egypt, goods were distributed by government allocation. In Rome, goods were distributed through the operation of the free market.[25] In Egypt, objects were priced by government fiat. In Rome, objects were priced by the market. The only difference between the Egyptian system and the Soviet system in the twentieth century is that in Egypt, the distribution was, by design, unequal in favor of the rulers, government officials, and religious elites; while in the Soviet system, the intent was an equal distribution of wealth (even though in practice, it looked more like the Egyptian model).

Some historians reject the notion that Rome was a capitalist economy. They are wrong. Their error is in having been influenced by Marxist ideas, which tend to identify capital with industrial assets and the machinery used in manufacturing. And finding no evidence of such, the easy assumption was that Rome was solely a consumer economy (forgetting that agricultural land, irrigation systems, warehouses, ships, and even roads are also capital).[26]

Rome's economic energy was provided by tradesmen and trading. Tradesmen, like carpenters and bricklayers, built the cities and aqueducts; weavers and tailors made the clothing; cobblers, the shoes; wagonmakers, the chariots and wagons; and so forth. Manufacturing, construction, and fabrication were definitely small-scale largely local operations. On the other hand, trading, especially overseas trading, was a big business, equal to that of the modern era. A good example is the annual shipments of wheat from Egypt, Sicily, Sardinia, and North Africa to fulfill the annual annona. This was the annual grain dole that fed the Roman urban population even when the city grew to over one million. The buyer was the state, but it involved going into the

---

25 Rome was not a democracy, not even close to it. Its political economy was structured to serve the interest of the ruling classes. The risk of discontent among the mass of the population was controlled by the grain dole (annona) to the people of Rome.

26 M. L. Finley, *The Ancient Economy* (Berkeley: University of California Press, 1999).

market and buying the grain, hiring the ships, insuring against storm damage in shipment, and arranging payment to sellers in distant ports. Hundreds of trading vessels plied the Mediterranean waters every day in season. All interregional and coastal shipping was in private hands.

But trading was not just carried out by sea and river; much was also done by land. Roman roads have been the wonder of history. Many remain in use today, two thousand years after having been built. All in all, Rome built over 250,000 miles of roads, of which fifty thousand miles were hard surface stone paved. Most of Rome's very considerable local, intrastate, and interregional commerce was carried out on these roads.

Rome's agricultural and product markets were large and well developed. Price equilibrium—allowing for transportation differences, especially for large-volume commodities like grain—prevailed throughout the empire. Also, in addition to the maintenance of predictable prices, Rome's well-developed long-distance trading operations gave rise to financial markets with a surprising degree of sophistication.

Peter Temin, probably the foremost student of Rome's market economy, has this to say about its financial markets:

> Financial intermediation was big business in first-century CE Rome and Italy. There was a wide range of institutions engaged in financial intermediation, including banks, brokers, partnerships, private individuals and some cities. Between them, they provided a wide range of services, including money changing, deposit accounts, mandated payments, transfers between accounts, credit for auctions, loans to clients and third parties, guarantees for contracts and legal appearances, and in the provinces, tax payments.[27]

---

27 Peter Temin, *The Roman Market Economy* (Princeton: Princeton University Press, 2013), 187–88.

CHARLES L. LADNER

Rome's was a laissez-faire economy. Rome also was a laissez-faire empire. It was generally true that so long as the provinces paid their taxes and tributes and the citizens of these subject nations and colonies paid a modicum of respect to Rome's gods and sacred traditions, they were free to operate in the economic sphere in any way they chose. This, of course, was completely contrary to the controlling theocratic way the kings, pharaohs, and Ptolemaic rulers governed the people and economy of Egypt. Yet even though Rome's political culture was based on the principles of free enterprise (analogous to the United States) and Egypt's was a closed autarchic system (analogous to the communist Soviet Union), both had a highly unequal distribution of income and wealth. Both were characterized by income and wealth distribution strongly biased toward an oligarchic elite. And both were organized, from the start, to funnel all possible income and wealth to such people. In the Roman Empire, the top 1.5% received 20.0% of the total annual income, and the next 10.0% of the population received another 20.0%. The remaining 88.5% of the populace shared about 60.0% of the empire's income, which left them impoverished, with annual money income roughly equivalent to 133.0% of a subsistence level of income. In this regard, the only difference between Rome and Egypt was that Rome had a sizeable middle class, comprising upward of 10.0% of the population, and Egypt did not. An estimated distribution of personal income in Rome during the first through the fifth century CE is shown on the following table:[28]

---

28 These numbers are very rough estimates. They are extrapolated from data in the following references, which, due to the paucity of quantifiable sources, are also inexact but represent the best available data at this point: Alan Bowman and Andrew Wilson, *Quantifying the Roman Economy* (Oxford: Oxford University Press, 2009); Walter Scheidel and Steven Friesen, "The Size of the Roman Economy and the Distribution of Income in the Roman Empire," in *The Journal of Roman Studies* 99 (2009): 61–91. Temin, op cit, 33, 102; Bryan Ward-Perkins, *The Fall of Rome and the End of Civilization* (Oxford: Oxford University Press, 2005).

Table 1. Inequality in Ancient Rome

Class	Population	% Pop.	Total Income in Sesterces	Income per Person	Equivalent US Income per Person
Senatorial	600	.0001%	180,000,000	300,000	$25,515,000
Equestrian	20,000	.029%	720,000,000	36,000	$3,061,000
Decurion	130,000	.186%	1,170,000,000	9,000	$765,450
Other Wealthy	899,400	1.285%	1,930,000,000	2.145	$182,500
Total Elite	**1,050,000**	**1.5%**	**4,000,000,000**	**3,810**	**$324,000**
Middle	**7,000,000**	**10.0%**	**4,000,000,000**	**571**	**$48,600**
Lower	**61,950,000**	**88.5%**	**12,000,000,000**	**194**	**$16,500**
Total	**70,000,000**	**100.0%**	**20,000,000,000**	**286**	**$24,300**

To put this data into perspective, the last column on the table shows the Roman currency expressed in 2018 US dollars. The translation from sesterces to dollars was derived by extrapolating from an assumed income level of 1.3 × subsistence that was thought to be the average of the mass of the Roman population and applying it to the 2019 United States Health and Human Services poverty guideline for one person. This allows us to gain some insight into the income relationship among classes. However, because it is based on publicly documented figures, it greatly understates the total income of all classes, especially the senatorial and equestrian classes who, in their ruling capacity, were beneficiaries of substantial cash and land from bribes and other like payments.

The whole purpose of this discussion of income inequality is to demonstrate that even in the best-run and presumably most fair society of the ancient world, income inequality was rampant. Moreover, with the fall of the Western Empire in 476 CE, the phenomenon of income (and wealth) inequality continued to expand with increasing differences between the small number of elite, composed of feudal rulers and high churchmen, and the mass of the increasingly impoverished rural

CHARLES L. LADNER

population. It was not until the fifteenth to sixteenth centuries that the trend began to reverse itself, propelled initially by the Protestant Reformation, which served to instill a sense of independence not only in religious matters but also in political and economic matters within the Protestant countries. Nonetheless, the distribution of income still remained highly unequal, but a lot less so.

CHAPTER FIVE

Aids to Analysis: Income and Inequality Data

O N THE PREVIOUS pages, I have referred to the Gini coefficient as an indicator of income inequality. The Gini coefficient is a measure of statistical dispersion and is the most commonly used data point in studies of income and wealth inequality. It is used to describe the extent to which the distribution of income or wealth among individuals, households, or groups deviates from a perfectly equal distribution. A Gini coefficient of 0 indicates perfect equality, where all members earn exactly the same amount. A Gini coefficient of 1 indicates a condition of absolute inequality, where one person earns all the available income. Unless otherwise noted, the income Gini coefficients in this book are based on purchasing power parity income and are displayed on the basis of income after taxes and all transfer payments.[29]

Most essays, papers, and books on the subject of economics use a variety of line, bar, and circular graphs to illustrate the characteristics of various economic systems, their growth patterns, and their inequalities. However, I believe graphs can lead to misinterpretation, so I prefer tabular presentations with simplified data because I think, if properly

---

29 Frequently, this data is calculated using income before taxes and transfer payments, which, in my view, tends to overstate the income disparities. Taxes in this context are taxes on income and do not include other forms, such as sales or VAT taxes. Transfer payments are payments made to individuals for health, welfare, and other social benefits. I believe this provides a more accurate presentation of income inequality because it is more representative of disposable personal income.

constructed, tables can convey information in a more accurate and analytical fashion. Therefore, in addition to the use of the Gini coefficient, you will find numerous tables but only a single graph in this book.

There are two tables that follow. Each one is organized into three groups: capitalist countries, socialist countries, and Nordic countries, which are capitalist but have a unique approach to social programs. Within each group, the countries are ranked according to their Gini coefficients from low to high. The Gini calculations of income are based on household income and prepared by the World Bank. So for example, Slovakia has the lowest Gini, which signifies a very equal distribution of income. After that is France, which is included as representative of the major European countries; South Korea and Japan are next as representatives of the Asian countries with strong, well-developed economies. They are followed by Russia, the United States, and China, which are the main subjects of this book, then we find Brazil, a country whose economic profile is similar to most of the Central and South American economies. And finally, there is South Africa, which can claim the crown as having the most unequal economy in the world.

Table 2, "Income and Inequality Data for Selected Countries," provides information regarding GDP per capita. This is not household income; rather, it is information regarding the whole economy, although it tracks reasonably close to household income. Also shown on this table are estimates of wealth per capita. The GDP data is current information (2018). But the wealth estimates are not current; they date from 2000. Unlike the data regarding income, which every nation collects assiduously because it is needed for taxation, there is no compelling need and there is considerable resistance to the collection of wealth information. Then follows the wealth Gini and the income Gini. Comparing these two indicators, it is interesting to note, for example, that while some countries have very low income Ginis, implying an exceedingly equal distribution of income, a few of these same countries are among those with the highest wealth Ginis and, thus, high inequality and high concentration of wealth. Surprisingly, the Nordic countries, along with

France, fall within this seemingly anomalous category, suggesting tax policies aimed at redistribution.

Table 3, "Percent Distribution of Personal Income by Quintile," is another way to visualize income disparities commonly used by economists. I find it useful to focus on the first column. It shows how much of the nation's personal income flows to the top 20%. So for example, in the United States, the top 20% of the population controls nearly 47% of the country's household income, whereas in the Nordic countries, the top 20% controls about 37%. I find it helpful to scan across the lines to get a sense of the actual levels of inequality implicit in the Gini.

Table 2. Income and Inequality Data for Selected Countries

	GDP Per Capita[30] 2019	Wealth Per Capita 2000	Wealth Gini[31]	Income Gini[32]
Capitalist Countries				
Slovakia	$32,763	$27,201	**0.629**	**0.252**
France	$46,184	$94,557	**0.730**	**0.316**
South Korea	$42,661	$41,439	**0.579**	**0.316**
Japan	$41,429	$124,858	**0.547**	**0.329**
Russia	$27,044	$14,762	**0.699**	**0.375**
USA	$62,683	$143,727	**0.801**	**0.414**
China	$16,117	$12,819	**0.550**	**0.385**
Brazil	$14,652	$16,519	**0.784**	**0.466**
South Africa	$12,482	$16,626	**0.763**	**0.630**
Socialist Countries				
Laos	$7826	No data		**0.364**
Vietnam	$8,041	$8,178	**0.682**	**0.357**
Nordic Countries				
Sweden	$53,205	$73,570	**0.742**	**0.288**
Norway	$63,663	$90,843	**0.633**	**0.270**
Finland	$48,621	$53,154	**0.615**	**0.274**
Denmark	$57,184	$66,191	**0.80**	**0.287**

30 2019 data expressed in 2017 US purchasing power parity dollars, accessed August 6, 2020, www.data.worldbank.org/indicator/NY .GDP.PCAP.PP.KD.

31 James B. Davies et al., The Level and Distribution of Household Wealth (Cambridge, MA: National Bureau of Economic Research, 2009), 56–60.

32 Gini index (World Bank estimate), www.data.worldbank.org/indicator/si.pov. gini?mosr recent value desc=false.

Table 3. Percent Distribution of Personal Income by Quintile-2015

	Top Quintile	Fourth Quintile	Third Quintile	Second Quintile	Bottom Quintile	Gini Coefficient
Capitalist Countries						
Slovakia	35.0%	23.2%	18.7%	14.6%	8.5%	**0.252**
France	40.9%	21.7%	16.7%	12.8%	7.9%	**0.316**
South Korea	39.1%	23.1%	17.5%	13.1%	7.2%	**0.316**
Japan	39.7%	22.7%	17.3%	12.9%	7.4%	**0.329**
Russia	45.3%	21.5%	15.2%	11.1%	6.9%	**0.375**
USA	46.9%	22.6%	15.3%	10.2%	5.0%	**0.414**
China	45.4%	22.3%	15.2%	10.6%	6.4%	**0.385**
Brazil	57.7%	19.5%	12.2%	7.4%	3.2%	**0.466**
South Africa	68.1%	16.5%	8.2%	4.8%	2.4%	**0.630**
Socialist Countries						
Laos	44.6%	21.0%	15.3%	11.5%	7.6%	**0.364**
Vietnam	42.5%	22.4%	16.3%	11.9%	6.9%	**0.357**
Nordic Countries						
Sweden	37.5%	22.8%	17.6%	13.9%	8.2%	**0.288**
Norway	36.5%	22.7%	17.7%	14.1%	9.0%	**0.270**
Finland	36.7%	22.4%	17.5%	14.1%	9.3%	**0.274**
Denmark	37.7%	21.8%	17.2%	13.9%	9.4%	**0.287**

Source: IndexMundi, "Income Distribution—Country Comparison," accessed July 30, 2020, www.indexmundi.com/facts/visualization/income-distribution.

CHAPTER SIX

Socialism

I N ITS MOST elementary sense, socialism is nothing more than an economic system with centralized coordination. It is one in which the productive assets are owned by the state and in which it is intended that all members share equally in all its economic resources. Pricing of goods and services is set by the central coordinating group.

The idea of socialism has been around a long time. Plato suggested a kind of socialism in his definition of a perfect political system in the *Republic.* But even earlier and in an even more fundamental sense, small tribal organizations from Neolithic times and before, in their sharing of resources, perfectly capsulized the idea of socialism.

Another example of nascent socialism was in medieval Western culture, where a good example of socialism has been the economic structure embodied by the Christian monastic movement. Since the second century up until the present day, millions of individuals have lived their lives in small socialist societies called monasteries, abbeys, or convents. Wealth, such as it might be, is shared equally. There is no individual ownership of property, there are no classes except as represented by the abbot or abbess, and no one has a claim on the assets of the monastery. While rivalries, jealousy, and inequalities frequently arise in such communities, I think it can be fairly said that for the most part, monastic life is a superb example of how socialism can actually work in real life.

Likewise, there have been numerous utopian communities, mostly in North America. Many of these communities, like the monastic communities, were bound together by a shared devotion to religious ideals or to the social programs of contemporary philosophers such as Robert Owen and Charles Fourier. Owen, in fact, established a utopian community in the United States called New Harmony in Indiana. The town still exists, but as a utopian society with all economic benefits distributed to each member of the community, it failed in 1827, less than three years after having been established on socialist principles. Owen's son, Robert Dale Owen, who continued to live in New Harmony, which became an important center of intellectual life in the middle years of the nineteenth century, had this to say about the failed experiment in his autobiography published in 1874:

> I do not believe that any industrial experiment can succeed which proposes equal remuneration to all men, the diligent and the genius and the drudge." Ever hopeful for the ultimate success of the socialist ideal, he goes on to say. "I speak of the present age; what may happen in the distant future it is impossible to foresee and imprudent to predict." Yet with a dose of reality, based on his own experience and that of his father, he says. "What may be safely predicted is, that a plan which remunerates all alike, will, in the present condition of society, ultimately eliminate from co-operative association the skilled, efficient, and industrious members, leaving an ineffective and sluggish residue in whose hands the experiment will fail, both socially and pecuniarily.[33]

Along with New Harmony, there were numerous utopian communities established in North America during the nineteenth century. Nearly all were based on socialist and egalitarian principles, although a few allowed for private ownership of property. Some were entirely secular, and some religious, but the one thing they had in common, along with their socialist point of view, was their short life. Here are some examples: Oberlin Colony (1833–1844), Brook Farm

---

33 Robert Dale Owen (1801–1877), *Threading My Way: Twenty-Seven Years of Autobiography* (London: Trübner & Co., 1874), 276.

CHARLES L. LADNER

(1841–1846), Fruitlands (1843–1844), Oneida (1848–1881), Amana Colonies (1850s–1932), and Shakers. The Shakers started in 1747 and continue today with a small community in Maine containing two elderly members. These and other similar communities flourished in the twenty years before the Civil War. Since then, they have steadily declined, both in numbers and population, most likely for the same reasons that initiated the collapse of the New Harmony community. The sole exception is the Shakers, a vibrant religious community held together and at the same time diminished by their pledge of celibacy, which requires a steady input of new adherents.

While the New World proved to be barren ground (until the 1930s) for socialist ideas or cooperative communities, it was an entirely different matter in Europe. Keeping in mind that in its most generalized terms, socialism refers to an economic system in which all goods and services are made available to all members of society in accordance with their needs while the production of such goods and services is performed in accordance with their physical and intellectual abilities and that in a pure socialist system, there is no private ownership of assets, no markets, no pricing of goods and services, and therefore no need for currency, it is easy to see that North America, with its vast undeveloped spaces and its availability of virtually free agricultural land, provided an outlet for the economic frustrations that remained pent-up and unfulfilled in Europe, while the socialist model provided to many Europeans an undeniably attractive alternative.

Theorists abounded, but without doubt, the most effective were Karl Marx and Friedrich Engels's, who together developed an advanced theory of socialism that they published in their 1848 tract *The Communist Manifesto*. This is truly a remarkable document. Starting with an analysis of history based on class struggle and the inevitability of the proletariat prevailing, with socialism being the penultimate step on the historic process leading to the final victory of the worldwide Communist revolution, they called for abolishing private property and centralizing all "instruments of production in the hands of the state."

They deemed all history and all cultural and social change was a function of the conflict between the oppressor class and the oppressed:

"freeman and slave, patrician and plebian, lord and serf, guild master and journeyman." And the latest versions of this class warfare entailed the challenge to dominance of the aristocratic feudal class by a newly empowered class of people called the *bourgeoisie*. These were the middle class of manufacturers, traders, bankers, and businessmen who—in the more advanced nations like England, France, and the Netherlands in the seventeenth through nineteenth centuries—were gaining control of the economic assets, productive capacity, and financial institutions, pushing aside the old aristocracy and then following the dialectic of history, emerging as the new oppressor class. The new class of oppressors—the *bourgeoisie*—were both the architects and product of the industrial revolution in manufacturing and the globalization of commerce made possible by new technologies, exemplified by the worldwide network of railroads developed in the early mid-nineteenth century, the advent of the oceangoing steamships, and the rationalization of the means of exchange, both in product and finance.

Emerging as their competitors and in conflict with the all-powerful *bourgeoisie* was the laboring class: the *proletariat*. These were the oppressed masses in the new economic world of the nineteenth century. They were the millions harnessed to the wheel: the coal miners, the millworkers, the laborers in the factories, the tenant farmers toiling in the countryside, the stevedores at the docks, etc.; all these millions of workers and their families constituted the *proletariat*.

Marx and Engels observed the regularity and the nature of business cycles and predicted that the entire machinery of the new *bourgeoisie* economic world would ultimately cycle into the overproduction of goods and service in quantities that the market could not absorb without destructive price competition. Moreover, in the minds of Marx and Engels, the capitalist bourgeoisie class also would overbuild manufacturing and distribution facilities to the point where the economic returns would approach zero. And, of course, the grossly underpaid masses of the *proletariat* certainly could not afford to buy the product. The consequence of all this being the bankruptcy, failure, and collapse of the entire *bourgeoisie* manufacturing and commercial structure. This was the cornerstone of Marx and Engels's analytical framework. They

CHARLES L. LADNER

described this phenomenon as the result of a fundamental internal contradiction of capitalism that would lead to its inevitable self-destruction. This then would allow for the emergence of the *proletariat* as the dominant force in society. They anticipated that the workings of this historical dialectic would lead initially to socialism, which, in turn, would soon dissolve into the "dictatorship of the proletariat," otherwise called communism.[34]

The Creation of the World's First and Most Successful Socialist State: The Union of Soviet Socialist Republics

In October 1917, the world's first socialist state was established by the violence of revolution and civil war in Russia.

For the purpose of this study, the Russian Revolution is the critical event in the analysis and the evaluation of the socialist model. Up to that point and, to some extent, even continuing on to the present, most of what passed as socialism was nothing more substantial than inchoate theories of philosophers about a "perfect" world interspersed by the establishment of a few short-lived small utopian villages. But this book is concerned only with actual real-world socialist economies and not with the array of pretentious and speculative abstractions building imaginary castles in the air. So the meanderings of dreamy intellectuals like Proudhon, Saint-Simon, Fourier, Bakunin, Negri, Kropotkin, and

---

34 Marx and Engels were correct in this prediction, except they underestimated the capacity of humans to adapt to changing circumstances. Certainly, the Depression of the 1930s was largely caused by overinvestment in capital goods and productive facilities whose output in both cost and quantity exceeded the purchasing power of the consumers. It is interesting to note that China today is embarked on this same path (see chapters 11 and 12).

the like have no relevance to this study because their ideas were never consummated in concrete reality.[35]

On the other hand, the hard-nosed realism of Lenin, Stalin, and their compatriots (as well as Mao, Pol Pot, and Castro) is what really matters in the study of socialism. These are the people who didn't just talk about it but actually did it. They gave life to the words of Marx and Engels.

The great contribution of Lenin was that he recognized that the only way to implement a socialist state was through an all-encompassing authoritarian governmental structure. Otherwise, the selfish interests of the displaced classes would undermine and destroy the socialist state before it even got started; and over time, the selfish interests of the citizenry would erode its effectiveness. Lenin's insight, which will be analyzed in biological terms later, has been demonstrated by the facts of history to be perfectly correct. There has never been a democratic socialist state. All socialist states that could claim even a modicum of success functioned on coercive totalitarian principles.[36]

During the chaos of Russia's October Revolution, Lenin and his minority party, the Bolsheviks, emerged on top. Unafraid to use violence and even terror, the Bolsheviks established themselves as the new leaders of Russia. They quickly moved to expropriate all properties of the crown, the church, and the gentry. Banks were taken into state ownership, and all loans to the czarist government were canceled. Many

---

35 Frequently, socialist ideas or programs are found incorporated within the political/legal structure of capitalist states. This does not make them socialist states. It is merely the adaptation of commonsense improvements in what otherwise is a capitalist economy. Examples of such improvements are government-sponsored retirement schemes (like Social Security in the United States), government-subsidized medical and health services as found in Canada or Germany, and trade unions as found everywhere.

36 Many on the Left who are sympathetic to socialism may have difficulty with my assertion that an autocratic or authoritarian political structure is necessary for socialism to function. This opinion is, in all likelihood, the logical result of a failure to distinguish between the socialist state (which is the focus of this book) and the presence of socialist institutions in states that are organized along nonsocialist lines, such as capitalism.

CHARLES L. LADNER

of the largest manufacturing facilities and mines were also expropriated. Lenin called for an end to the war and entered into peace negotiations with Germany, which culminated in the Treaty of Brest-Litovsk in which Russia surrendered control of the Baltic states, Belorussia (until 1923), and Ukraine (until 1919). But most importantly, for the purpose of cementing Lenin's control, the politburo established a security police force known as the Cheka. This governmental department was the instrument by which terrorism was promoted such that it permeated all levels of society to firmly enforce the Bolshevik's totalitarian regime with Lenin at its head.[37]

Lenin's initial economic moves so destabilized the economy that the party had to back off and regroup. It did so by promulgating a modified socialist approach called the New Economic Plan (NEP) that permitted private enterprise among small businesses and the agricultural community (comprising about 80% of the population). The NEP turned things around and got the economy back on a solid footing.

Lenin, who had been seriously ill since late 1921, died in January 1924. During the period of Lenin's illness, his principal associate, Joseph Stalin, consolidated his power; and upon the death of Lenin, Stalin became the head of the politburo and the unchallenged leader of Russia. In 1928, Stalin, a true believer in what became known as Marxist-Leninist socialism, initiated the first five-year plan, emphasizing the development of heavy industry. About the same time, he initiated the collectivization of the agricultural sector. All privately owned properties were expropriated and incorporated in a vast system of industrialized farms known as collective farms. Millions were displaced. Many migrated to the cities seeking work in the rapidly growing heavy industrial sector, but many in the rural regions, estimated to be upward of seven million people, died in the resultant famine. Also, during the 1930s, Stalin's security forces arrested about 1.6 million people who were deemed insufficiently loyal to the state and its socialist policies. It is estimated that approximately seven hundred thousand of these unfortunate people

---

37   Robert Service, *Comrades: A History of World Communism* (Cambridge: Harvard University Press, 2007), 70–72.

were executed. As the 1930s drew to a close, Russia was a fully operative socialist state. It was the first and most successful entity of its kind.[38]

Private ownership of all economic assets and resources was eliminated. Everything was owned by the people acting through the state. All services, education, childcare, health, communication, transportation, housing, etc. were provided by the state. Banking, foreign trading, and financial services were state monopolies. And the glue that held it all together and made it function was the authoritarian government of Joseph Stalin—a despot running the government and controlling the instruments of coercion, which were mainly the state security forces and the military. Stalin's rule spread terror and fear throughout the Russian population, and that was the critical ingredient to making socialism work.

Russia came through World War II with horrendous, unthinkable losses, but in the end, Russia was not just victorious but also was celebrated as a unique socialist example to the world.

---

38   Ibid.,142–145.

CHARLES L. LADNER

CHAPTER SEVEN

The Collapse of the Soviet Union

THE SOVIET UNION emerged from World War II confident and strong, challenging the West on all fronts and determined to aggressively promote the international sweep of communism. Russia absorbed the Baltic states and drew the republics into a codependent union. In Eastern Europe, where Russia's armies displaced the Germans, they stayed and oversaw the conversion of the Eastern European countries to socialist satellites of the Soviet Union. Elsewhere during the next decade, China, North Korea, much of Southeast Asia, and many of the developing nations in Africa, all adopted socialism as the governing principle of their economies, typically accompanied by oppressive autocratic rule, without which socialism cannot exist. By 1985, the advance of socialism had an air of inevitability about it, with nearly 40% of the world's population living in socialist states.[39] This was a total of almost two billion people living in the USSR, its Eastern European satellites, China, North Korea, Cuba, parts of Southeast Asia, and many of the former European colonies in Africa.[40] Yet within a decade, by 1995, socialism throughout the world had evaporated. It was found to be a mistake and was uniformly rejected in favor of the free enterprise model championed by the West, which had produced dramatically higher living standards than were found in the socialist countries. Thus the 40.0% of the world's population that had previously embraced socialism dwindled to a mere 1.5%.

---

39 Thomas Lansford, *Communism* (New York: Cavendish Square Publishing, 2007), 9–24, 36–44.
40 Tony Wood, "Organization over Ideals: The Global History of the Communist Party," *The Nation* (March 25, 2019).

In 2020, only one socialist nation remains: Cuba. Some of the former socialist states still identify themselves as socialist, or as communist, but by every measurable standard, all are now free-enterprise capitalist economic entities, though authoritarian governments (the indispensable condition of socialism) still hang on in a few places.

However, in the late 1990s, notwithstanding the virtual disappearance of socialism throughout the world, the Soviet Union still stood strong; so on December 25, 1991, the entire world was stunned into disbelief when the Soviet Union's president, Mikhail Gorbachev, resigned the office and declared it extinct. The next day, the Supreme Soviet voted itself out of existence, thereby terminating Russia's identification as a socialist state. Symbolically, the Soviet flag was lowered and the Russian tricolor of czarist days was raised in its place.

How could this have happened? For forty-five years since the end of World War II, the Soviet Union had competed on seemingly equal terms for world dominance with the United States and the other Western democracies. Along with the US, it had become one of the only two world superpowers. It developed nuclear weapons and the intercontinental missiles to deliver them. It put the first man in space. Its military technology was equal or better than that of the West. Its jet aircraft, tanks, and submarines were probably the world's best. And its five-million-man armed forces made the Soviet Union a nation to be feared.

However, as we have since learned, the breakdown of the Soviet Union had deep roots, extending back in time to its inception as a socialist state. In the post–WWII years, all this expansive national power and stature was fueled by a strong economy. Immediately after the war, Soviet industry and agriculture did very well. Living standards improved, and the military might was unexcelled. It is now apparent that by 1985, the Soviet Union reached its economic and political zenith; but from that point on, it ran out of steam. And the story of the economy then became an accelerating downward spiral. The numbers tell the tale. During its most prosperous period, 1950–1973, the Soviet Union's average growth rate in per capita GDP was 3.6% per year.

Then from 1974 through 1984, per capita GDP growth stagnated at an annual rate of .9% per year. Finally, for the next six years leading up to its dramatic collapse, the Soviet Union's average per capita growth was a *negative* 1.3% per year.[41]

The diminishing growth in the 1970s and the negative growth in the 1980s were not missed by Soviet leaders; neither was it missed by economists in the West. As early as 1970, Yale University economist Martin Weitzman noted that

> during the early years the Soviet economy could grow extremely fast by piling up productive capital at rates that were unprecedented in history. But by now (1970), the accumulation of capital has outstripped labor by a wide enough margin that the drag due to diminishing returns has cut into output growth ... the days of relying on capital formation alone for producing 10 to 15 per-cent increases in industrial output would appear to be over.[42]

Starting in 1928, the Soviet Union's economic policy was to collectivize the agricultural sector, which resulted in creating a large pool of excess laborers, while at the same time embarking on an accelerated program of extensive industrial development—building mills, factories, forges, and even new industrial cities, thus absorbing the excess laborers unneeded by the collectives. This policy, enabled by the coercive nature of the Stalinist regime, worked very well. But as Weitzman later pointed out, adding capital to replace labor without new technology inevitably would result in diminishing returns and slow or even negative growth. Moreover, in the later years, the sclerotic rigidity of the Soviet Union's embedded system of centralized control had the effect of misallocating

---

41   Numa Mazat and Franklin Serrano, *An Analysis of the Soviet Economic Growth from the 1950's to the Collapse of USSR*, accessed April 1, 2020, www.centrosaffa.org/public/bb6a675-6bef-4182-bb89-339ae1f7e792.pdf.

42   Martin Weitzman, "Soviet Postwar Economic Growth and Capital Labor Substitution," *American Economic Review* 60 (1970): 676–92.

resources, discouraging innovation, and disincentivizing productivity of both the agricultural and industrial labor forces.

In the late 1980s and early 1990s, as the Soviet Union's economy began to crater, other economists weighed in. Among them was Martin Gur, writing in the late 1980s for the RAND Corporation, who echoed Weitzman's observation regarding the failures of the Soviet Union's industrialization policy and added (1) the drag caused by defense spending, which, by definition, is a zero growth investment; (2) the increasing complexity of the economy, which rendered centralized planning not only useless but also a significant barrier to growth as it created confusion and supply backlogs; and (3) a weakening of the employee incentive system.[43]

In 1994, looking back with the perspective of hindsight, William Easterly and Stanley Fischer, writing for the World Bank, generally agreed with the Weitzman thesis that the declining marginal product of capital was a principal structural cause of the Soviet Union's failing economic performance, but they also suggested that the burden of defense spending was problematic. Moreover, they also implied that the increasing breakdown of worker discipline compounding on itself ever since the death of Stalin in 1953 and the consequent abatement of state terrorism could have been an important contributing factor. But above all, they concluded "that it was the planned economic system itself that was disastrous for long run economic growth in the Soviet Union."[44]

Weitzman, Gur, Easterly and Fischer, and many others analyzed the collapse of the Soviet Union as a function of embedded long-term structural infirmities. The next two studies look at the immediate cause of the catastrophe.

Andrei Shleifer and Robert Vishny, writing for the Brookings Institution in 1991, immediately before the final collapse of the entire Soviet house of cards, attributed the economic problems to "repressed inflation" that resulted in drastic shortages of medicine, food, and

---

43 Martin Gur, *Soviet Economic Growth 1928–1985* (Los Angeles: RAND Center for the Study of Soviet International Behavior, 1988), v–vii.

44 William Easterly and Stanley Fischer, "The Soviet Economic Decline: Historical and Republican Data," *The World Bank Policy Working Paper* 1284 (1994).

staples, especially in the cities and other places where people relied on the state system of distribution. The state held prices stable, while the true prices, as reflected by the farmers market and the black market, were about four times higher. The worst distortion was in pharmaceuticals, which were mostly imported from the West. They were priced in the free market at nineteen times the state prices. Naturally, when such price differentials exist, the state stores get nothing, shortages result, and public discontent rises to an extreme degree. The rate of year-over-year inflation in the free markets (cooperatives, collectives, foreign imports) was 9.5% in 1989, 29.0% in 1990, and 71.0% in the first quarter of 1991. The problem was not getting better.[45]

Finally, we have the words of an insider, Yegor Gaidar, who was a senior official in both Gorbachev's and Yeltsin's governments and served for a short time as prime minister (1991) and later as finance minister (1991–1992). In brief, while he acknowledges that repressed inflation was the regime's most serious political problem, it was the lack of hard currency caused by failures in the oil and gas sector that was the immediate precipitating factor causing the empire's bankruptcy in December 1991.

As disclosed by Gaidar, it was for at least a decade from the late 1970s forward that Russia was unable to produce the quantity of grains, vegetable oils, meat, and other staples sufficient to feed its population. Russia also imported most of its pharmaceuticals and much of the high tech equipment required to operate the petroleum industry. The only solution was to buy these essentials from the Free World (i.e., Asia, Europe, and North America).

However, by the late 1990s, Russian currency and, ultimately, Russian credit were not accepted anywhere in the world outside the Soviet bloc. Yet foreign hard currency was required. The sole source of such foreign exchange (meaning dollars) to pay for these items was through the export of oil and gas. However, as is normal in the oil and gas industry, output was falling each year as existing wells run down

---

45 Andrei Schleifer and Robert W. Vishny, "Reversing the Soviet Economic Collapse," *Brookings Papers on Economic Activity* 2 (1991).

the normal production decline curve. Typically, in producing oil fields, new wells are drilled every year, if only to maintain production at a level base. But the Soviets got behind the curve and lacked the funds to drill enough new wells to maintain production. The central planners in Moscow really did not understand this until it was too late. Somehow, year after year, they thought oil production would rise simply because they put it in the budget. They might have got away with that strategy when it came to collective farms or heavy-industry internal sectors that could play games with their numbers as they had learned so well in the past, but it did not work that way in the domain of international trade.

At a meeting on September 17, 1990, of the Soviet Council of Ministers, Chairman Nikolay Ryzhkov[46] said that "oil production in the period from 1975 to 1990 fluctuated within a range of 500–600 million tons, while capital investments grew from 3.8 billion rubles to 17 billion rubles in 1991 (this was in a discussion of the plan for 1991). The number of wells required to produce 1 million tons grew from 16 in 1975 to 165 in 1990. The number of meters drilled grew tenfold. And oil production was beginning to fall, despite all that."[47]

To provide insight into the confusion and frustration encountered by Soviet leadership in the late 1980s to early 1990s as they attempted to find their way through the morass brought about by the socialist system, the following is a transcript of the meeting of the senior leadership, the "brain-trust of the central planning."[48] This group comprised the Soviet Union's most senior leadership. Only Mikhail Gorbachev was senior to these men. Ryzhkov, as chairman of the Council of Ministers, was the equivalent of prime minister; Maslyukov, who was in charge of Gosplan (the agency responsible for central planning), had recently been first deputy chairman of the Council of Ministers; Voronin was also a first deputy chairman of the Council of Ministers; and Ryabyev and Sitarian were both deputy chairmen of the Council of Ministers.

---

46 Ryzhkov served as prime minister under Mikhail Gorbachev from 1985 to 1991 and later was a candidate for president opposing Boris Yeltsin.

47 Yegor Gaidar, *Collapse of an Empire: Lessons for Modern Russia*, trans. Antonina W. Bous (Washington, DC: Brookings Institution Press, 2007).

48 Ibid.

The following are excerpts from the transcript of the meeting on September 17, 1990. (I have boldfaced some of the more telling comments.) In reading this, keep in mind that Russia needed 580–600 tons of annual petroleum production to survive:

Comrade Ryzhkov: **What do we do with 547 tons, how will the country live?**

Comrade Ryabyev: For domestic consumption there will be 467 tons.

Comrade Ryshkov: But still, what needs to be done to get to 580, as we had discussed at first?

Comrade Ryabyev: Those are very difficult numbers. We need to increase drilling and introduce 25–26 thousand new wells. There has to be a sharp increase.

Comrade Sitarian: How much money is needed for these things?

Comrade Ryabyev: Approximately 800 million rubles in convertible currency.

Comrade Ryzhkov: Your task is to find a way to get out of this situation.

Comrade Ryabyev: We have looked into all of this. The first variant was presented to you in July—to redistribute resources in the country. **There are simply no other resources ... None.**

Comrade Sitarian: The general situation is such that **if we export** (only) **60 million, then we put the relationship with other countries in an extremely difficult position.** That is, if today 34 million tons goes to hard currency (exported), that leaves 26 million for all the Eastern European countries plus Finland, India, Cuba, and so on ... if we are losing 20 million now, that means our hard currency resources for next year will be 14 million. I feel that signing for 60 million in exports should not be done ... **The point is that we cannot fail to deliver oil to certain countries. If we stop at** this number, it means a complete collapse inside the country and with many countries …

Comrade Maslyukov: We understand that **the only source of hard currency is, of course, oil,** so I will make this proposal, I feel that we must approach those proposals made by the geologists and take the most determined measures to achieve additional oil production … Second, I would think that all the necessary resources that we named should definitely be purchased from foreign firms … **I have the presentiment that if we do not make all of the necessary decisions now, then we may spend next year in a way that we haven't even dreamed of … Things can end most critically in the socialist countries. This will lead us to a real crash, and not just for us, but for our entire system.**

Comrade Voronin: I can only say that the oil industry has never before been in this situation, not even in 1985. It has reached the point that we may even fear not getting 500 million tons of oil, if things continue this way … I understand that **if we can't get at least 570 million tons, we will let down everything, the socialist countries, our food production and machine building** … The really hurtful thing is that oil is at a good price and it will keep rising, while we will be producing less and less. Therefore we must give the socialist countries the minimum for hard currency, and **reduce the domestic demand** as much as possible …

Comrade Ryzhkov: We need guarantees from Vneshekonombank (The Soviet's international bank), **and it can't give them** … We have to make the decision to go for 547 million tons, and of that there will be only 60 million tons for export, both to socialist countries and to capitalist countries, which will ruin everything … If we don't find the formula now to save

CHARLES L. LADNER

the oil and gas industry, we won't get even 547. There has to be a definite system; either we force them to reach the goal, or we will stay on the downward slide. I am concerned that we have already met several times this year and we can't handle the situation. We have to stay at 560 million tons and we have to devote all our material resources to it ... **I see that if there is no oil, there is no economy ...**

These men all knew that the Soviet Union was locked out of the international credit markets because of its inability to service existing debt and its failure to pay for past deliveries of imported goods. They also knew that the only source of hard currency (dollars) was through the export of petroleum to Western countries. And finally, they knew they needed hard currency to (1) buy much-needed grain and foodstuffs to feed the urban population, (2) buy Western oil drilling and other petroleum technology for new wells and pipelines to arrest the relentless decline in oil and gas production, and finally (believe it or not), (3) in a plea of pitiful self-deception, some of these supposedly rational people thought the Soviet Union could and should still provide support to socialist dependencies like Cuba and the few remaining socialist satellites.

"We may spend next year in a way we haven't even dreamed of ... This will lead to a real crash, not just for us, but for our entire system." Yuri Maslyukov's prediction proved to be eerily correct. His somewhat foreboding observation was made at the meeting that was held in September 1990 regarding the numbers forecasted for 1991. And just as they all dimly perceived, the Soviet leadership did spend 1991 in a way they hadn't ever dreamed of. The Soviet Union, and with it the idea of socialism, imploded in December 1991, and the entire system descended into chaos.

CHAPTER EIGHT

Lessons regarding the Viability of Socialism

T HE PRIMARY CONCEPT of state socialism is to create a society in which everyone shares equally in all the economic benefits. There are many variants to this idea. It is conceivable that there could even be a socialist state in which private property is the dominant form of ownership. But the characteristic without which socialism cannot exist is the *equal* distribution of both wealth and income to all members of the community or political body, with a centralized body setting all prices and allocating resources. Failing that test, it is *not* socialism.

The Soviet Union came pretty close to that ideal—close enough that any fair-minded evaluation of the Soviet state from at least the late 1930s to the mid-1980s would have to conclude that it definitely met the criteria and, in fact, represented the quintessence of socialist theory in practice.

Indeed, the Soviet Union checked all the boxes in the socialist playbook. Private ownership of property was virtually eliminated. The state owned all the agricultural and industrial means of production. There was no such thing as unemployment. All who could work were employed by the state, and those who could not work (for reasons of health or age) were supported by the state. The state provided all health care. It provided all childcare and education. It set up government-run retail establishments in which all merchandise and products were price-controlled in order to assure stable retail prices and eliminate the effect of inflation on ordinary citizens. (The state absorbed all the inflationary costs as a liability on its own balance sheet, a policy that was to have devastating consequences after the collapse of the system and the move toward privatization.)

But most of all, as the embodiment of the socialist ideal, the signature accomplishment of the Soviet Union was to achieve near perfection in the equal distribution of income and wealth throughout all strata of society. Here is historian Walter Scheidel on this topic:

> Driven entirely by political intervention, further leveling occurred in the decades after World War II. Farm incomes, which had been extremely low, were allowed to rise more quickly than urban wages were, and the latter were leveled by raising lower wages, narrowing wage differentials, and increasing pensions and other benefits. Policy inspired by communist ideology particularly favored manual workers: the wage premium for all nonmanual workers fell from 98 percent in 1945 to 6 percent in 1985, and technical-engineering personnel experienced a similar drop. White collar wages declined to well below the mean for manual workers. Even at times of substantial economic growth, despotism was capable of greatly flattening and reshaping income distribution.[49]

The upshot of all this was that the Gini coefficient between 1968 and 1985 ran between 0.27 and 0.28 for the entire nation.[50] Considering the hierarchical inequalities unavoidable in large industrial and governmental bureaucracies, this is a level of equality that probably approaches the optimum for a large sophisticated industrial economy.

But all this progress toward socialist perfection came at a very large cost.

---

49 Walter Scheidel, *The Great Leveler: Violence and the History of Inequality from the Stone Age to the Twenty-First Century* (Princeton: Princeton University Press, 2017), 221.
50 Ibid.

Already noted are the seven million deaths from famine in rural areas resulting from the coercive movement to achieve collectivization of agriculture and the 1.6 million executions later in the 1930s in the interest of "political correctness." Of almost equal horror was the continuously sustained sadism of Stalin's police state terror that eviscerated the soul of the Russian people in the sole interest of coercing their subservience to the dictates of state socialism. Stalin, as is well documented, was a true believer. He had the ultimate power of life and death, and he exercised it without reservation.

In this book's analysis of the socialist economy, its point of departure is an economic system's correspondence with the most fundamental human need of selfishness. Keeping that in mind, it seems reasonably clear that the socialist system presented serious difficulties. History has shown that socialism cannot exist without the discipline of an authoritarian government to compel mass behavior contrary to human instinct. Other than careerism within the bureaucracies of industry or government service, the system itself puts rigid limits on an individual's legitimate consummation of selfish desires. Thus, illegitimate (sometimes illegal) means are pursued. Consider this: of the 280 million Soviet citizens in the mid-1980s, probably half to three-quarters were in this box. That would be 140–210 million people.

How do they resolve this? The only possible correctives are to either sublimate instinctual drives or to seek relief in illegitimate behaviors. Such things as absenteeism became increasingly common from the mid-1950s death of Stalin through the collapse in 1991, while during this same period, alcoholism grew to become a national crisis. But most of all, it was in the small undetectable liberties people took in their daily work routines, by withholding their efforts and preserving both their physical energies and their self-respect, that did the damage. Within this closed system, the risk to the worker of being terminated and out of a job was so low as to be almost nonexistent. So, as became stunningly evident, with no personal exposure, the natural response of a worker's always-present instinctive selfishness was that universal systematic malingering became the cultural norm. Thus, in tiny increments—putting in just a little bit less work effort, being just a little less attentive to the quality of output, taking longer breaks, arriving late and leaving earlier—things that are hardly noticed in an individual and hardly worth a supervisor's admonishment became commonplace. However, when these miniscule inefficiencies became habituated among the 140–200 million workers and became a normal constituent of everyday work habits for thirty-five years, the cumulative impact on the economy was devastating.

To illustrate the impact, here are some hard-to-believe examples provided by Yegor Gaidar:

> The Soviet Union mined eight times as much iron ore as the United States. That ore yielded only three times as much pig iron, and the pig iron only twice as much steel as was produced the United States. Finally from that steel it was able to produce machines worth roughly the same as those produced in the United States.
>
> The use of raw materials and energy in the production of each final product was, respectively, 1.6 and 2.1 times greater than in the United States. The average construction time for an industrial plant in the USSR was more than ten years, in the United States, less than two years. In manufacturing per unit, the USSR used 1.8 times more steel than the United States, 2.3 times more cement, 7.6 times more fertilizer, and 1.5 times more timber. The USSR produced 16 times the number of grain harvesters, but harvested less grain and became dependent on grain imports.[51]

Throughout the postwar years, the period called the Cold War, the principal goal of the Soviet leadership was to achieve levels of personnel income at parity with the West. It never succeeded. A major embarrassment for the Soviets was that socialism failed. Somehow, the economic system promoted to be the unique source of worker income improvement could not function without repression. The following

---

51   Gaidar (2007).

information, compiled and published by the World Inequality Lab, illuminates this matter.

From 1870 through 1930, the ratio between national income per adult in Russia and Western Europe (ratio) averaged approximately 35%. This meant that the average income of a Russian citizen during the czarist period and the early years of socialist rule was only one-third of the average adult income in France, Germany, and Great Britain. Then in the next period, from Stalin's ascension to power to his demise in 1953, with his propensity toward the use of terror and of tyrannical coercion to force compliance with the socialist model, the ratio improved. It rose dramatically from 35% to approximately 63%, clearly demonstrating that with socialism, oppression works. Finally, from the mid-1950s through the collapse of the Soviet Union in 1991, with a relaxation of the repressive activities of the Stalin era and significant governmental intervention in putting off the effects of inflation, the ratio neither improved nor declined but was artificially supported at about 63%, thus, strongly suggesting that absent repression, socialism fails—a fact that was made perfectly clear after the collapse, when the buried inflationary and other economic problems exploded into chaos.[52]

Socialism in China: Been There, Done That!

Socialism lasted seventy-four years in the Soviet Union before it was abandoned. It lasted twenty-eight years in China before it was abandoned. Between the two, there was an interesting parallel. Both countries began their romance with socialism as feudal agrarian societies. Both were brought to socialist perfection by tyrants who achieved their ends through terror and mass murder. Stalin, in the Soviet Union, was credited with seven to ten million deaths; and Mao, in China, was responsible for an estimated thirty to forty million deaths. Both leaders were true believers. Their moral compass and resultant policies were shaped by their ideological certainties. The people of both countries

---

52 *World Inequality Report 2018*, issued by World Inequality Lab at the Paris School of Economics.

suffered greatly. Their literacy and health care improved, but their sense of personal security was shattered by successive waves of persecution. What good would it do to provide your family with a nice standard of living only to have some devoted socialist operative break into your home, accuse you of bourgeoisie behavior, and shoot you on the spot? Yet this was the terror under which most Chinese lived during Mao's reign.

By the time of Mao's death, 95% of China's arable land had been organized as government-owned collectives, and virtually all small and large business operations, a total of eight hundred thousand firms, were in governmental hands. Moreover, during the socialist period, the forced leveling of wealth and incomes had resulted, by the mid-1950s, in moving the Gini coefficient from 0.40 to 0.31 and then to 0.23 on the eve of the country's move to privatization.[53]

Following the death of Mao in 1976, the repression eased, but it was a period of political and economic uncertainty until two years later when Deng Xiaoping (Deng) emerged as the new paramount leader. Deng ruled for fourteen years, and during that time, he renounced Mao's two disastrous initiatives: The Great Leap Forward (1958–1962) and The Cultural Revolution (1966–1976), both of which, while intended to affirm China's ideological purity, had the effect of not only causing immense suffering and countless deaths but also of degrading whatever economic progress the Chinese people made since the 1950s. Deng, in contrast to Mao, was able to distinguish between economic activities and political activities. His nuanced approach to governance was gradually accepted by the dominant Communist Central Committee, allowing China to become a free market participant in the world economy while simultaneously governing itself along Marxist-Leninist lines (absent the economics). Maintaining the fiction that it was a socialist state was important to the hard-line Marxists, while to the rest of the world, by its economic behavior at home and intense participation in the world's capital markets, there was little doubt that by the 1990s, China had made the transformation from socialism to capitalism.

---

53   Scheidel (2017), 223–227.

Even its current (2019) Gini coefficient of 0.385, along with the fact that 45% of the nation's personal income flowed to only 20% of the population and the further reality of China's astounding number of billionaires (799), which is the highest in the world and exceeds even the United States (585), graphically attests to its abandonment of any pretext of socialism.[54]

---

54 The data on billionaires is from Hurun Global Rich List (Shanghai: Hurun Research Institute, February 26, 2020), accessed June 2, 2010, www.hurun.net/EN/Article/Details?num=775CERAE8F8.

CHARLES L. LADNER

CHAPTER NINE

Capitalism and Free Enterprise

A T THE START of chapter 7, I broadly defined socialism as

> an economic system that functions with centralized coordination in which the productive assets are publicly owned by the state and in which it is intended that all members share equally in all its economic resources and benefits, with pricing and allocation of goods and services set by the central coordinating group.

In contrast, I would broadly define capitalism as

> an economic system with decentralized coordination in which the productive assets are privately owned and operated for a profit and in which members share in the benefits only to the extent they own the assets or are employed by those who own the assets, with pricing and allocation of goods and services set by the market.

It is central to my analysis that capitalism is the system to which all other economic systems default. Socialism is an artificial construct intended to improve on the pre-capitalism that spontaneously arises in primitive human society or the more evolved economic forms such as feudalism or classical capitalism.

A critical element of capitalism is profit. Goods and services are produced and priced to generate profits that may be distributed to the owner of the business for current consumption or reinvested in the business to fuel future growth. Unlike socialism, which has no inherent mechanism for growth, the capitalist system has a growth mechanism at its heart; for when the business owner elects to defer current consumption and reinvest in the business, he/she will expect that the future earnings will increase in proportion to the amount reinvested. When this occurs at thousands of firms within a national economy, the economy, or the state, will experience a rate of economic growth (and all that implies in terms of tax revenue and employment opportunities), commensurate with the average earnings rate of reinvestment multiplied by the amount of the reinvestment.

However, antecedent even to the notion of profit is the existence of markets largely free of governmental or other exogenous interference so that goods and services may be efficiently and fairly priced and allocated. Historically, free markets are difficult to attain. In the seventeenth and eighteenth centuries, governments imposed tariffs and trading restrictions in an effort to divert income as an alternative or a supplement to direct taxation. The British Navigation Acts applied to tobacco trade in the American colonies is a good example. This law required that tobacco grown in the colonies be sold only to British buyers, priced by British buyers, and transported only on British vessels. Once arriving in Great Britain, the government took control and determined where the product would be sold, giving preference to foreign sales so as to increase foreign exchange and extract sales tax revenues from people other than British citizens. This meant that the prices paid to the growers in the colonies were severely depressed in comparison to world market prices. It not only gave rise to smuggling but also, more importantly, was a crucial source of discontent, especially among the Southern colonies, leading up to the American Revolution.

This is a good example of mercantilism, an economic theory based on the notion that trade is a zero-sum game, which attempted to tilt the monetary gains to one's own country. Both the British and the French were particularly adept at extracting value from this practice. But in the late eighteenth century, when such economists as Adam Smith and David Hume demonstrated that trade was not a zero-sum game, the idea was gradually abandoned in favor of free trade.

CHARLES L. LADNER

By the late eighteenth century, side by side with the flourishing of the industrial revolution, the entire structure of the classical capitalist system emerged—a structure centered on the factory system combined with the belief, as an article of faith, in the concept of self-regulating free markets monetized with currencies based on the gold standard.

Then throughout the nineteenth century and into the early twentieth century, the wealth and economic progress of Europe, North America, and the rest of the developed world seemed to expand without limits. In these parts of the world, science and technology brought astounding benefits not just in general knowledge but also in living standards, with such things as city water and sanitation services, gas cooking, electric lighting, central heat, automobile, paved roads, telegraph, telephone, motion pictures and radio, air travel, elevators enabling high-rise buildings, professionalization of medical education and practice, new medicines, advancement in public health, and all the benefits of modern life that we are all too happily familiar.

However, not all parts of the world shared in this bounty. Asia and parts of Latin America did not catch up until the mid-twentieth century, and the Middle East is still behind. But even in the West, all was not smooth sailing. There were bumps along the road, and the biggest bump occurred in the first half of the twentieth century, as the whole system came unraveled with the agonies of two world wars separated by the devastation of a worldwide economic depression. It seemed to many as though the progress derived from capitalism was a cruel illusion.

Analyzing this economic and societal implosion from the perspective of the mid-1940s, economic historian Karl Polanyi discerned what appeared to be the fundamental flaw in the capitalist system.

He argues in his influential 1944 book, *The Great Transformation*,[55] that in order to organize and expand the factory system that was developing in the eighteenth century, it was necessary to fit it (the factory system) into the already prevailing market system. But markets require

---

55 Karl Polanyi, *The Great Transformation: The Political and Economic Origins of Our Time* (Boston: The Beacon Press, 1957).

interchangeable objects to trade. The linkage, economists will maintain, are the three elements essential to the factory system (and to capitalism itself), which are termed the factors of production. They are material, labor, and money. But to fit these things into the market system, they must be transformed into commodities. That way, by commodifying them, they can be broken down into interchangeable units and traded on an exchange or other market with ease. This, of course, is easy or even natural for money and material, but not so much for labor. For *labor* is just another word for people, and to commodify people and organize them as a factor of production is, in the words of Polanyi, "to change the organization of society itself" so that social organization of humans becomes "an accessary of the economic system."[56]

This was accomplished in Britain by the passage of the Poor Law Amendment of 1834, which redefined social stratification as follows:

> The legislation segregated the "poor into physically helpless paupers whose place was in the workhouse, and independent workers who earned their living by laboring for wages. This created an entirely new category of the poor, the unemployed, who made their appearance on the social scene. While the pauper, for the sake of humanity, should be relieved, the unemployed, for the sake of industry, should *not* be relieved."[57]

Thus, labor, as a factor of production and by law, was commodified to become an instrument of market and priced by wages. Moreover, the clear implication of this law in both code and practice was that the labor content of value was separated from any human welfare considerations and priced solely by the transactional give-and-take of the market.

This social tsunami first began to appear in the mid-eighteenth century and crested with Britain's poor laws in the 1830s. It prevailed, as a way of legally defining the rights of the employer and employee for a century, but not without protest and political resistance. On the

---

56   Ibid., 75.
57   Ibid., 224.

CHARLES L. LADNER

one hand, with the legal clarification of labor's place within the free market, the Industrial Revolution blossomed throughout the Western world and produced the economic superabundance that characterized its civilization. However, notwithstanding the economic efficiency of pricing the work of human labor as a transactional commodity, by situating a depersonalized labor force within the free market to be traded just like any other commodity, a century of anger and strife bedeviled the capitalist free market system—the consequence of which was a revolutionary reversal in the standing of the laboring class wherein the entire structure of society and politics was changed by the extension of universal democracy to people of all classes and genders, thus enabling labor an equal seat within the market.

Power to the people, as it were, meant governmental intervention within the market in the form of ever-increasing regulation and the encouragement of strong labor unions. In the United States, the Sherman Antitrust Act (1887) regulated business combinations and controlled monopolies; the Interstate Commerce Act (1887) was initially concerned with railroad rates but had long since been the foundational authority underpinning the regulation of all commercial activities extending beyond a single state; the Pure Food and Drug Act (1906) regulated meatpacking, food processing, and drugs; the various state regularity acts (1910–1920) limited the rates and profits earned by monopolized gas and electric companies; and the Clayton Act (1914) removed trade unions from jurisdiction under the Sherman Act, thus paving the way for union organizations to become national in scope and finally redressing the injustices implicitly codified in the American and British law.

Governmental regulation effectively removed labor from the market and also intervened in so many other areas that the so-called self-regulating free market of nineteenth-century classical economics ceased to be the organ of social control, as it had been throughout the century. By the 1930s, in the United States, France, Benelux, and the English-speaking countries, the reform of the system and the disintegration of the market as the sole determinant of economic justice were well underway. In Germany, Italy, and Spain, the inadequacy of the market-driven economy to assure job security and its blindness to fundamental human needs resulted in the sudden rise of fascist autocracies that promised favorable treatment of the masses and—for the most part—delivered on those promises, at least until they delivered their people into the killing fields of war.

In all this, Polanyi was not only a good observer of what was happening in his own time but he also was quite prescient when it came to discerning the postwar trends of economic organization, with Britain, Italy, France, and Germany adopting an extensive filigree of socialist programs to provide for the laboring class, mostly at the expense of the wealthy. "Within the nations," he says, "we are witnessing a development under which the economic system ceases to lay down the law to society and the primacy of society over that system is secure … In effect, the disintegration of a uniform market economy is already giving rise to a variety of new societies."[58]

Consistent with Polanyi's expectations, socialism, already firmly established in the Soviet Union, became widely accepted among academics, reformers, and populist politicians as the solution to the type of economic injustice identified with nineteenth-century capitalism—an ideology commonly identified as one of the root causes of the devastating political and social evils of the first half of the twentieth century. To such people, nothing was more attractive and more rational than to replace the messy imprecision of a market-driven economy with a political and economic system based on planning and managed by highly educated experts. Thus, even Great Britain and the European capitalist countries elected labor/socialist parliamentary majorities and adopted centralized government-provided services for such things as health care, housing, employment, and a whole variety of other human needs. Meanwhile, the Eastern European nations gave themselves over to an all-enveloping socialist form of government as satellites of the Soviet Union, while, at about the same time, the newly emergent former Asian and African colonies of the now enervated European powers

---

58 Ibid., 249, 252.

embraced with great enthusiasm the whole gospel according to Marx, Engels, and Lenin.

Polanyi was certainly correct, at least in the short run. By 1976, it has been reliably estimated that 34.9% of the world's population (1.4 billion people) were living in socialist states. This was truly a remarkable achievement for the socialist movement. In 1944, only the Soviet Union, with 6% of the world's population could be properly called a socialist state.[59]

Yet by 1991, socialism had all but evaporated from the world's landscape, with only Cuba as the last remaining holdout. The reason for the disappearance of socialism was exactly as described earlier: it simply does not work in practice! Socialism sounds great in the textbooks, but it inevitably fails in the laboratory of real life. The fact that socialist states in Eastern Europe and Africa lasted as long as they did was entirely the result of their being financially supported by the Soviet Union, so when the Soviet Union crashed in 1991, it took with it the whole worldwide web of socialism.

On the following pages are two tables showing the gross domestic product (GDP) per capita of the socialist and former socialist countries for the period 1950–2016. Also shown, for reference purposes, is the same data for the United States and Sweden. The GDP numbers are expressed in constant 2011 US dollars to eliminate distortions from inflation. The data is presented by decades, and the decades during which various countries were identified as socialist states are shaded in gray. These were the years, known as the Cold War, when the socialist countries (led by the Soviet Union) and the democratic capitalist countries (led by the United States) were engaged in vigorous competition.

During these years, the oft repeated objective of the Soviet leaders was to catch up and surpass the United States. And in this regard, the Soviets did credibly well in the areas of space and military technology. They also excelled in the propaganda war, as demonstrated by the rapid

---

59   CIA memorandum addressed to the chief, White House support staff, dated March 9, 1976, accessed April 28, 2020, www.cia.gov/library/readingroom/docs/DOC_0000969777.pdf.

expansion of socialism from the 1950s through the 1980s. But in terms of national wealth and standards of living, they fell woefully short.

To illustrate this latter point, the second table expresses the GDP per capita of each of the socialist and former socialist countries as a percent of the GDP per capita for the United States. The figures speak for themselves. Nothing, it seems to me, more graphically portrays the sheer inadequacy of the whole socialist program than this comparison. This was the laboratory of real life, and socialism failed.

The effect of this extended subpar economic performance was evident to all. As the years passed, a steady stream of reports from Western newspapers, radio, and television, along with books and magazines smuggled and surreptitiously circulated, made the people of these closed socialist societies painfully aware of the breadth of the disparity in the living standards of ordinary people. Some of these countries, like the Soviet Union, could not even produce enough food to feed their own people. The inevitable result was the catastrophic collapse of socialism, which occurred in the early 1990s.

What this data categorically demonstrates is the unqualified superiority of capitalism as a generator of national wealth. What it does not reveal, however, are the deep internal self-destructive inconsistencies of capitalism over the long term. That will be a topic of the last chapter.

CHARLES L. LADNER

Table 4. Gross Domestic Product Per Capita (PPP) of Selected Socialist and Former Socialist Countries 1950–2016 (Note: Self-identified socialist years shaded gray.)

Country	Year Begin	Year End	1950	1960	1970	1980	1990	2000	2016
United States			$15,241	$18,058	$23,958	$29,613	$36,982	$45,887	$53,015
Sweden			$8,816	$11,391	$18,133	$20,491	$26,364	$36,374	$44,371
Socialist and Former Socialist States									
Albania	1944	1992	$1,478	$2,142	$2,957	$3,501	$4,099	$5,183	$11,285
Bulgaria	1946	1990	$2,922	$5,153	$8,447	$10,591	$10,874	$8,671	$17,953
Cambodia	1975	1991	$553	$769	$742	$923	$997	$1,289	$3,307
China	1949	1980	$757	$923	$1,291	$1,690	$2,460	$4,071	$12,320
Congo	1970	1993	$1,181	$1,396	$1,647	$2,888	$2,409	$2,727	$4,310
Cuba	1959	Present	$3,841	$4,360	$4,335	$5,979	$6,864	$4,882	Unavailable
Czechoslovakia	1948	1990	$6,390	$9,551	$12,376	$15,630	$17,045	$16,153	$30,118
Hungary	1949	1989	$2,654	$4,507	$7,039	$11,289	$12,097	$14,757	$24,047
Laos	1975	Present	$621	$688	$758	$931	$1,459	$1,994	$6,324
Mongolia	1924	1992	$669	$900	$1,210	$1,722	$3,319	$2,737	$11,105
Poland	1952	1989	$3,141	$4,125	$5,683	$6,221	$7,476	$13,207	$26,002
Romania	1965	1989	$951	$1,853	$3,581	$6,165	$6,868	$7,430	$18,913
Russia (USSR)	1917	1990	$5,676	$8,386	$13,275	$16,948	$19,941	$7,633	$18,105
Ukraine	1919	1991				$9,376	$9,204	$11,208	$19,896
Vietnam	1945	1976	$890	$1,080	$994	$1,076	$1,200	$2,243	$6,031
Yemen	1967	1990	$1,055	$1,116	$1,424	$2,652	$2,630	$3,068	$2,199
Yugoslavia	1945	1992	$1,251	$2,118	$3,595	$5,848	$5,342	$9,770	$16,361
Average GDP/Capita of Socialist States			**$2,697**	**$3,758**	**$4,847**	**$6,397**	**$7,798**	**$4,882**	**$14,267**
Percent of USA			17.7%	20.8%	20.2%	21.6%	21.1%	10.6%	26.9%
Russia % of USA			37.2%	46.4%	55.4%	57.2%	53.9%	16.6%	34.2%

Table 5. Gross Domestic Product Per Capita of Selected Socialist and Former Socialist Countries as a Percent of the United States 1950–2016 (Note: Self-identified socialist years for each country shaded gray.)

Country	1950	1960	1970	1980	1990	2000	2016
United States	$15,241	$18,058	$23,958	$29,613	$36,982	$45,887	$53,015
Albania	$1,478	$2,142	$2,957	$3,501	$4,099	$5,183	$11,285
%	9.7%	11.9%	12.3%	11.8%	11.1%	11.3%	21.3%
Bulgaria	$2,922	$5,153	$8,447	$10,591	$10,874	$8,671	$17,953
%	19.2%	28.5%	35.3%	35.8%	29.4%	18.9%	33.9%
Cambodia	$553	$769	$742	$923	$997	$1,289	$3,307
%	3.6%	4.3%	3.1%	3.1%	2.7%	2.8%	6.2%
China	$757	$923	$1,291	$1,690	$2,460	$4,071	$12,320
%	5.0%	5.1%	5.4%	5.7%	6.7%	8.9%	23.2%
Congo	$1,181	$1,396	$1,647	$2,888	$2,409	$2,727	$4,310
%	7.7%	7.7%	6.9%	9.8%	6.5%	5.9%	8.1%
Cuba	$3,841	$4,360	$4,335	$5,979	$6,864	$4,882	Unavailable
%	25.2%	24.1%	18.1%	20.2%	18.6%	10.6%	
Czechoslovakia	$6,390	$9,551	$12,376	$15,630	$17,045	$16,153	$30,118
%	41.9%	52.9%	51.7%	52.8%	46.1%	35.2%	56.8%
Hungary	$2,654	$4,507	$7,039	$11,289	$12,097	$14,757	$24,047
%	17.4%	25.0%	29.4%	38.1%	32.7%	32.2%	45.4%
Laos	$621	$688	$758	$931	$1,459	$1,994	$6,324
%	4.1%	3.8%	3.2%	3.1%	3.9%	4.3%	11.9%
Mongolia	$669	$900	$1,210	$1,722	$3,319	$2,737	$11,105
%	4.4%	5.0%	5.1%	5.8%	9.0%	6.0%	20.9%
Poland	$3,141	$4,125	$5,683	$6,221	$7,476	$13,207	$26,002
%	20.6%	22.8%	23.7%	21.0%	20.2%	28.8%	49.0%

CHARLES L. LADNER

Romania	$951	$1,853	$3,581	$6,165	$6,868	$7,430	$18,913
%	6.2%	10.3%	14.9%	20.8%	18.6%	16.2%	35.7%
Russia (USSR)	$5,676	$8,386	$13,275	$16,948	$19,941	$7,633	$18,105
%	37.2%	46.4%	55.4%	57.2%	53.9%	16.6%	34.2%
Ukraine				$9,376	$9,204	$11,208	$19,896
%				31.7%	24.9%	24.4%	37.5%
Vietnam	$890	$1,080	$994	$1,076	$1,200	$2,243	$6,031
%	5.8%	6.0%	4.1%	3.6%	3.2%	4.9%	11.4%
Yemen	$1,055	$1,116	$1,424	$2,652	$2,630	$3,068	$2,199
%	6.9%	6.2%	5.9%	9.0%	7.1%	6.7%	4.1%
Yugoslavia	$1,251	$2,118	$3,595	$5,848	$5,342	$9,770	$16,361
%	8.2%	11.7%	15.0%	19.7%	14.4%	21.3%	30.9%

Source for tables 4 and 5: Jutta Bolt, Robert Inklaar, Herman deJong, and Jan Luiten van Zanden, *Maddison Project Database, Version 2018*, "Rebasing Maddison: New Income Comparisons and the Shape of Long-Run Economic Development," Maddison Project Working Paper 10 (Groningen Growth and Development Centre, University of Groningen, 2018).

Note: The best way to read table 4 is to select a country and scan across the data year by year. This makes it easy to get a sense of how each nation's economy has performed over time, always keeping in mind that the data measures performance relative to the United States. So if the ratio is relatively unchanged, one can infer that the subject economy is growing at about the same pace as the United States, but it is not gaining and, thus, remains at the same subpar status as at the beginning.

Then to see what can happen to the same economy under capitalism, one should compare the last year under socialism (i.e., the last entry in the gray area) with its performance in 2016. In many cases, the improvement will be striking, for the same economy that went nowhere as a socialist state shows meaningful, sometimes massive, improvement when socialism is discarded.

CHAPTER TEN

Types of Capitalism: Liberal Meritocratic Capitalism

A FTER A CENTURY of competition with socialism in all its many variants, it is now perfectly clear that apart from one or two insignificant little economies, capitalism has become the world's sole economic system. Feudalism is gone. Mercantilism is gone, and now socialism is gone. What remains is capitalism, but it comes in many flavors, and it comes with considerable baggage.

Bearing in mind that capitalism—along with its handmaiden, the free market—is the only economic system in the history of the world that is uniquely the product of human instinct, we should be fully aware that its success is not a surprise but rather has always had a degree of inevitability about it. However, if capitalism is truly the embodiment of the most elementary of human instincts—self-preservation and reproduction expressed as selfishness or greed—then it should be equally evident that whatever defects are attached to these genetic instincts will also be carried over to its derivative. Capitalism is an unequaled force for good insofar as it has the potential for eradicating the suffering of worldwide poverty. But because it is rooted in selfishness at its very heart, it has the potential for unbounded evil. After all, no one has ever claimed selfishness to be a virtue.

Accordingly, what I am trying to do in this work is to develop an understanding of how society can address the challenge of channeling the human instinct of self-interest to good purposes without suppressing its singular motivational quality. The exploration of this question is the underlying theme of everything that follows in this book. And, in truth, this same theme, though not explicit, has been foundational in all that has gone before.

Economist Branko Milanovic´, in his recently published study *Capitalism, Alone The Future of the System that Rules the World,* has identified two distinct types of capitalism that are rising to prominence in the twenty-first century: liberal meritocratic capitalism and political capitalism. He sees the United States as the archetype of the former and China of the latter.[60]

Liberal meritocratic capitalism is, in his view, an intrinsic derivative of nineteenth-century classical free market capitalism, with its emphasis on innovation and freedom from state interference. However, it is not a direct sequential offshoot of classical capitalism, but rather it has more the character of a return to the classical model.

The Development of Twentieth-Century Social Democratic Capitalism

As noted earlier, the nineteenth-century model contained within itself the source of its own destruction, because it could function only by reducing human work to the level of a transactional commodity to be traded on the so-called self-regulating free market. Such legally sanctioned degradation of the human person became the catechism of the nineteenth-century economic culture. But notwithstanding its demonstrated success as an instrument of wealth creation, it was bound to fail, as it ultimately did. The growing awareness of inequality and economic oppression eventually fueled popular movements that brought about new democratic forms such as universal suffrage, powerful independent trade unions, and raft of regulatory reforms designed to redistribute economic, health, and welfare advantages from the capitalist class to the working classes. Such movements, though punctuated over time, dominated the economic scene for much of the early to mid-twentieth century. Milanovic´ calls this social

---

60 Branko Milanovic´, *Capitalism, Alone: The Future of the System that Rules the World* (Cambridge: The Belknap Press of Harvard University, 2019), 2–11.

democratic capitalism. It began to emerge just before the First World War (1914–1918), reached fruition in the years following the Second World War (1939–1945), and since then, in many variants, has been capitalism's principal form, having been finally adopted by the former socialist countries as their economies crumbled during the 1980s and 1990s.

Social democratic capitalism has been good for the world. According to the World Bank, worldwide gross domestic product per capita (spearheaded by China and India, both of whom fully adopted capitalism by 1990) expressed in current purchasing power parity international dollars was $4,290 in 1990, rising to $11,313 in 2018.[61] This was an annual compound growth rate of 3.7%, or said differently, it meant that the world's economy on a per capita basis was routinely producing more than 2.5 times the amount of goods and services in 2018 than it had been able to produce in 1990. A very good way to understand the impact of this on people's lives is to see the improvement in worldwide poverty data, where it may be seen that the number of people in poverty in 1990 was 1.9 billion, or 36% of the world's population. But by 2015, the number in poverty had declined to 734 million people and, at that point, represented 10% of the world's population.[62]

Indeed, this is good news; however, regionally, there is a wide variation. China and India account for almost one billion of those moving out of poverty, while Sub-Saharan Africa experienced an increase of those in poverty, mainly as a consequence of wars and extreme corruption.[63] For example, approximately 70% of the population in the Congo and 70% of the population in Nigeria live in poverty, while in Madagascar, approximately 63% of the population live in poverty.[64]

Notwithstanding the seemingly intractable corruption and military strife in Sub-Saharan Africa and Central America, the rest of the world avoided such disruptions and succeeded in growing their economies while

---

61 Source: World Bank national accounts data and OECD National Accounts data files. License: CC BY-40.

62 Source: www.Worldbank.org/en/topic/poverty/overvies, accessed May 4, 2020.

63 Source: www.devnit.org/publications/poverty-trends-global-regional-andnational/, accessed May 4, 2020.

64 Source: CIA World Factbook, 2020.

CHARLES L. LADNER

simultaneously establishing strong public welfare programs. These programs varied widely in scale and coverage but generally included forms of universal health care, retirement benefits, unemployment benefits, university education, and income supplements. For Western Europe, Canada, the United States, and Japan, the social benefit programs, which in some cases were preexisting, were intensified immediately in the wake of World War II. For China it was in the 1980s, and for Eastern Europe, India, and Korea, the dynamic in which economic growth is coupled with strong social programs became evident in the 1990s. In all cases, the economic system that made this possible was the adoption of the concept of private ownership of economic assets that is central to the capitalist model and the rejection of the socialist idea of state ownership of the means of production and the state control of product pricing and resource allocation.

The following exhibit, table 6, provides additional data to measure the status of the world's economies. It does so against two standards: (1) the United States, which is generally considered the world's leading economy, and (2) the Organisation for Economic Co-operation and Development (OECD), which comprises thirty-seven of the most advanced economies, excluding Russia, China, India, and Brazil. The GDP data is expressed in purchasing power parity (PPP) current international dollars. The World Bank describes such international dollars as having the same purchasing power a US dollar has in the United States, ruling out local exchange rate and price and other differentials, thus making the dollars equivalent among countries in terms of what they can buy.

On this basis, one can see that the growth rates for the world, the OECD economies, and the United States have been hovering around 3.9–4.0% per year, while China ran in the 11–12.0% range for two decades, only to slip to just under 9.0% in recent years, possibly reflecting President Xi's inclination to assert more governmental influence over the economy than had been present during the past twenty years since the death of Mao. Regarding China, one can also see that in 1990, its GDP per capita, the legacy of Mao's ideological blindness, was truly abysmal. In fact, it was less than that of Sub-Saharan Africa, while today, after discarding Mao's destructive philosophy, it is nearly five times greater. Moreover, China is on the path to equaling or surpassing the United

States and will likely do so unless Xi and his associates, who pine for the days of political and economic autocracy, wreck the train—an outcome for which there is a distinct probability.

Finally, in terms of inequality differentials, the GDP per capita for the OECD countries consistently runs about 73% of that of the United States, while China and the world now are about 29%, and Sub-Saharan Africa is about 6%.

Table 6. Regional GDP Per Capita, Regional Growth in GDP Per Capita, the Percent of the United States GDP Per Capita 1990–2018

	1990	2000	2010	2018
US: GDP/Capita	$23,889	$34,513	$48,416	$62,794
% Growth		4.29%	2.92%	3.29%
OECD: GDP/Capita	$16,682	$25,237	$35,248	$45,623
% Growth		4.23%	3.40%	3.28%
% of USA		*69.46%*	*72.73%*	*72.65%*
World: GDP/Capita	$5,798	$7,986	$12,876	$17,948
% Growth		2.94%	4.89%	3.87%
% of USA		*21.98%*	*26.57%*	*27.79%*
China: GDP/Capita	$987	$2,936	$9,304	$18,236
% Growth		11.51%	12.22%	8.78%
% of USA		*8.08%*	*19.20%*	*29.04%*
Sub-Saharan Africa				
GDP/Capita	$1,718	$1,983	$3,224	$3,985
% Growth		1.46%	4.98%	2.68%
% of USA		*5.46%*	*6.65%*	*6.35%*

Source: World Bank national accounts data. License: CC BY-4.0.

The Emergence of Liberal Meritocratic Capitalism

In 1932, two Columbia University professors, attorney Adolf Berle and economist Gardiner Means, both of the Law School, published a breakthrough study of what they discerned as a newly emerging structure of capitalism. This work, *The Modern Corporation and Private Property*,[65] was a legal and statistical analysis of the rapidly growing organization of economic activity under the umbrella of the public corporation, which they accurately described as embodying the concentration of wealth coupled with the dispersion of ownership. This, they point out, had the practical effect of separating control from ownership. That is to say, in the large public corporation, into which an ever-increasing percentage of the US economy was being absorbed, the shareholders, who were nominally the owners, had relinquished their control of the assets to the directors and managers of the firm (the control group) and thereby limited themselves to changes in share value and to receiving only the immediate monetary benefits of ownership, which came to them in the form of dividends.

Buying and selling assets, merging with other firms, hiring and firing employees, setting wages, contracting for goods and services, coordinating and relating activities with and for governmental authorities, entering into partnerships and into trade agreements—all these activities and many, many others are among the traditional legal attributes of ownership, yet under the then new corporate organization of assets, such activities were disconnected from ownership. However, in an interpretation of this new definition of property rights, Berle and Means suggest that in eliminating the traditional rights of the owners, "the control groups (directors, management, and investment bankers) have, rather, cleared the way for the claims of a group far wider than either the owners or the control group. They have placed the community in a position to demand that the modern corporation

---

65   Adolf Berle and Gardiner Means, *The Modern Corporation and Private Property* (New York: The Macmillan Company, 1932).

serve not alone the owners or the control group, but all society … It remains only for the claims of the community to be put forward with clarity and force."[66]

In 1932, Berle joined Roosevelt's Brain Trust, where his influence was instrumental in constructing the regulatory framework that not only corrected the confusion that evolving corporate governance brought about by the separation of ownership from control but also provided the philosophical foundation for intervention on behalf of "all of society." The resulting New Deal legislation set the tone for capitalism in the United States throughout the twentieth century and was decisive in establishing, by example, a conceptual skeleton on which many social democratic capitalist economies were built throughout the world in the period following World War II.[67]

The transition from nineteenth-century classical capitalism to the more disciplined and regulated social democratic form was a slow process, mainly because it entailed a conversion of the general population from a then pervasive belief in the doctrine of individual self-reliance to one of mutual responsibility. The first glimmerings appeared in Germany in the 1880s where legislation providing for health insurance, disability allowances, and old-age pensions first appeared in various schemes that obliged the employer and the government to share with the employee the cost of these services.

Progress was slow. Although in the United Kingdom and other parts of Europe labor parties were organized and became an effective political force early in the twentieth century, legislative progress lagged. In the United States, an example of the prevailing attitude, substantially unchanged since the beginnings of the Industrial Revolution, may be seen in the report by Secretary of Labor W. B. Wilson to President Wilson detailing the nature of labor strife that affected industrial production in World War I, during which time he chaired the president's Mediation Commission:

---

66 Ibid., 355–356.
67 The most important legal structures were the Glass-Steagall Act of 1932, the Securities Act of 1933, the Securities Exchange Act of 1934, the Public Utility Holding Company Act of 1935, and the Investment Company Act of 1940.

Too often there is a glaring inconsistency between our democratic purposes in this war abroad and the autocratic conduct of some of those guiding industry at home.[68]

Modern large scale industry has effectively destroyed the personal relation between employer and employee— the knowledge and cooperation that come from personal contact. It is therefore no longer possible to conduct industry with employees as individuals. Some form of collective relationship between management and men is indispensable.[69]

In 1935, shocked by the catastrophe of the Great Depression, the US Congress enacted the National Labor Relations Act (Wagner Act), which guaranteed the rights of workers to organize and to carry out collective bargaining. In Germany, France, and England, such rights were not gained until the 1940s.

The hegemony of the capitalist class was not really broken until sixty years had passed between Bismarck's social laws in the mid-1880s and the adoption in Europe and the United States of the principles of social democratic capitalism. And while a new form of capitalism, liberal meritocratic capitalism, is now becoming visible, it will likely take a comparable length of time for it to become firmly established.

Branko Milanovic´, who coined the term, pins a considerable part of his argument for the emergence of liberal meritocratic capitalism on the phenomenon first observed in the 1980s of a change in the ratio of labor to capital in national income accounts.[70] To be more specific, the labor-capital ratio refers to an economic convention in which the

---

68   W. B. Wilson, "Extract from Report of President's Mediation Commission in Baruch, Bernard," *American Industry in the War: A Report of the War Industries Board*, transmitted March 3, 1921 (New York: Prentice-Hall Inc., 1941), 342.

69   Ibid., 343.

70   Milanovic´ (2019), 14–15.

national income account (GNI or GDP)[71] is divided between labor and capital. Labor is usually defined to include, wages, benefits, and the labor component of proprietor's income. Capital includes corporate profits, net interest, rental income, and the annual amortization of fixed asset costs, otherwise known as depreciation.

What is important about this relationship is that the percentage of labor in national income has been long thought to be reasonably stable. In fact, from 1900 to 1952 in the United States, it fluctuated within the narrow range of 69.2% to 76.5%.[72] And in a different period, it averaged about 70% from 1947 to 1983, at which point it began to decline, falling to about 64% in 2013.[73] There are numerous variants to this ratio that depend on the composition of the data (should CEO income be included in labor? how should proprietor's income be split? are stock options compensation or capital?). One well-regarded study complied by University of Chicago economists Loukas Karabarbounis and Brent Neiman not only confirmed the decline in labor but also proposed that its principal cause was the effect of advances in information technology that allowed firms to substitute capital, in the form of technology, for labor.[74] Technological change is a common explanation for the decline in the labor share, but there are other equally credible explanations for all or part of the decline, such as globalization in which laborers from lower wage countries displace employees in higher wage economies, or offshoring—or even the threat of it, which puts pressure on wages—or the decline in union density or even the perverse effect of higher levels

71   Organisation for Economic Co-operation and Development (OECD), "The Labour Share in G20 Economies, Report Prepared for the G20 Employment Working Group, Anatalya, Turkey, 26–27 February 2015," 14.

72   Gale D. Johnson, "The Functional Distribution of Income in the United States, 1850–1953," in *The Review of Economics and Statistics* 36, no. 2 (1954): 178, accessed May 11, 2020, doi: 102307/1924668.

73   Olivier Giovannoni, *What Do We Know about Labor Share and the Profit Share?* (Annandale-on Hudson, NY: Levy Economics Institute, 2014), 8–9, accessed May 10, 2020, http://www.levyinstitute.org/pubs/wp_805.pdf.

74   Loukas Karabarbounis and Brent Neiman, *The Global Decline of the Labor Share*, NBER Working Paper 19136 (Cambridge: National Bureau of Economic Research, 2013), accessed May 12, 2020, http://www.nber.org/papers/w19136.

CHARLES L. LADNER

of unemployment insurance that can induce people to choose leisure rather than work.[75]

Milanovic´ points out that this rebalancing of the scales in favor of capital versus labor implies that capitalists are becoming more important and thus increasing their political power—a trend seen before in nineteenth-century classical capitalism, but not in twentieth-century social democratic capitalism. Moreover, he puts forth the observation that those who derive income from capital are usually rich and are few in number, thus further intensifying the already evident tendency within the US economy toward income inequality.[76]

One pivotal development observed by Milanovic is that unlike previous forms of capitalism—when the rich capitalist class collected income, it was almost entirely from passive earnings on their assets—now what is increasingly seen is that the same person who is a high earner from capital is often and simultaneously an exceedingly high earner from wages. Think, for example, of Jeff Bezos, Mark Zuckerberg, or the Silicon Valley and Seattle billionaires. All are earning huge sums from their jobs while also earning as much or more from their passive assets. The same phenomenon may be seen on Wall Street among investment bankers or on Main Street among CEOs.

This is the meritocratic part of liberal meritocratic capitalism. Most of these people who combine high capital income with high labor income are self-made. They achieved their wealth and income on their own merit.

Much of Milanovic's work is intuitive and not firmly supported by an abundance of quantitative data. Even the assertion that there is a growing identity of wage-rich people with capital-rich people has weak statistical support, except as regards France where he relies in Thomas Piketty's excellent analysis demonstrating that capital as a source of income among the top percentile fell from 22% in 1900 to 9% in the mid-1940s and then to about 7% by 1990, with a modest rebound to 11% in 2014. He amusingly called it the fall of the rentiers, because

---

75 OECD (2015), 9–10.
76 Milanovic (2019), 15–16.

over much of the same long period (1910–1990), the share of wages in the top percentile has remained stable at 6%. Thus, the ratio of capital to labor in national income accounts changed so substantially that it almost disappeared.[77]

However, notwithstanding Piketty's compelling argument, what holds true in France may not necessarily hold true in the United States, especially when attempting to explain the opposite effect. In France, the income share of the top 1% peaked at about 24% in the late 1920s and then, coincident with the Great Depression and World War II, fell precipitously, reaching approximately 8% in 1945, and has been since hovering within a range between 8 and 11%. Therefore, if the labor share in the national accounts remained stable, then almost the entire fall of the top 1%, may be explained by a decrease in the capital share. Given the historical background, it should be evident that the radical change in the composition of the labor-capital ratio was occasioned by the enormous political and economic disruptions of an extended depression and a lengthy destructive war. However, in the United States, during the 1980–2013 period, no such disruptions occurred. So the comparison with France is not entirely apt. On the other hand, it can be credibly argued that in France, absent the near confiscatory estate taxes and the existence of an annual capital tax on all owned assets, the 1980–2013 period might have had a similar proportionate increase as in the United States.

In developing his concept of liberal meritocratic capitalism, Milanovic cites six essential attributes that differentiate liberal meritocratic capitalism from earlier forms. They are presented in tabular form.

77   Thomas Piketty, *Capital in the Twenty-First Century*, trans. Arthur Goldhammer (Cambridge, MA: Harvard University Press, 2014), 342–5.
Bertrand Garbinti, Jonathon Goupille-Lebret, and Thomas Piketty, *Income Inequality in France: Economic Growth and the Gender Gap* (London: CEPR, 2020), accessed May 14, 2020, www.voxeu.org/income-inequality.

Table 7. Key Features of Classical, Social Democratic, and Liberal Meritocratic Capitalism (from Milanovic')

	Form of Capitalism	Classical Capitalism	Social Democratic	Liberal Meritocratic
	Representative Economy	UK before 1914	US and Europe after WWII	US in Early Twenty-First Century
1	Rising share of capital income in net product	Yes	No	Yes
2	High concentration of capital ownership	Yes	Yes	Yes
3	Capital-abundant individuals are rich	Yes	Yes	Yes
4	Capital-income rich are also labor-income rich	No	No	Yes
5	Rich (or potentially rich) marry each other	Yes	No	Yes
6	High correlation of income between parents and children	Yes	Yes	Yes

Source: This table is taken directly from Milanovic' (2019), 14.

As shown in this table, the correlation of labor-income rich with capital-income rich is the unique characteristic of liberal meritocratic capitalism. It is that that sets it apart from all previous forms of capitalism.

If, as Milanovic' insists, there is an identity of the capital-income rich with the labor-income rich such that they are the same people (no. 4 on table 6), if people who own significant amounts of capital are also rich (no. 3), if there is a high concentration of capital ownership (no. 2), and if this concentration has been increasing in recent years (no. 1), then these items should be independently quantifiable and readily confirmed.

Starting first with the question of rising and concentrated capital ownership in the United States, Edward N. Wolf reports in a recent and highly credible study of household wealth that aggregate household net worth increased from approximately $26 trillion in 1983 to $84 trillion in 2016 (expressed in constant 2016 dollars). This was an increase of $58 trillion and was almost entirely distributed to the top 20% of the population. This top quintile gained $56.5 trillion in increased net worth, which was 97.0% of the total. Meanwhile, over the same time period, the remaining 80.0% of the population, representing 101.1 million households, received only $1.5 trillion, or 3.0% of the total.[78]

Predicated on this data, we can agree with Milanovic that not only has the aggregate household income increased substantially but also the increase has been almost entirely concentrated at the top.

But there's more. When we segment the top 20%, we find even more concentration. Another NBER paper, this one provided by Emmanuel Saez and Gabriel Zucman (2014), decomposed the top 10% for the year 2012.[79] This kind of information, regarding the very wealthy, is notoriously difficult to access, but as the output of an extraordinary work product, the authors were successful in capitalizing income tax data to derive the wealth held by the 1.0%, the 0.1%, the 0.01% and the 0.001%. The findings from the Saez and Zucman paper are reproduced below:

78   Edward N. Wolff, *Household Wealth in the United States, 1962 to 2016: Has Middle Class Wealth Recovered?* NBER Working Paper 24085 (Cambridge, MA: National Bureau of Economic Research, 2017), calculation from data on tables 3–5.
79   Emanuel Saez and Gageiel Zucman, *Wealth Inequality in the United States since 1913: Evidence from Capitalized Income Tax Data*, NBER Working Paper 20625 (Cambridge, MA: National Bureau of Economic Research, 2014).

CHARLES L. LADNER

Table 8. Thresholds and Shares in Top Wealth Groups, 2012

Wealth Group	Number Families	Wealth Threshold	Average Wealth	Wealth Share
Full Population	160,700,000		$343,000	**100.0%**
Top 10%	16,070,000	$660,000	$2,560,000	77.2%
Top 1.0%	1,607,000	$3,960,000	$13,840,000	**41.8%**
Top 0.1%	160,700	$20,600,000	$72,800,000	**22.0%**
Top 0.01%	16,070	$111,000,000	$371,000,000	**11.2%**

Source: Emmanuel Saez and Gabriel Zucman, *Wealth Inequality in the United States since 1913: Evidence from Capitalized Income Tax Data*, NBER Working Paper 20625 (Cambridge, MA: National Bureau of Economic Research, 2014), table 1.

The numbers on this table speak for themselves, but what is not shown is the magnitude of the change in recent years. For example, in 1983, the bottom 90% held 35% of the nation's net assets; but by 2012, this had fallen to 23%. Meanwhile, at the same time, the top 10% went from 65% to 77%. Moreover, during this time frame, the top 1% went from 25% to 42%, the top 0.1% went from 9% to 22%, and believe it or not, the top 0.01% (16,070 households) more than tripled their share of the nation's net assets from 3% to 11%.

This data clearly reinforces Milanovic's assertion of an increasing concentration of *wealth*. He also maintains a similar position regarding *income*. And this, too, is independently confirmed.

As to the distribution of income among the population hierarchy, a study issued in 2018 by Thomas Piketty, Emmanuel Saez, and Gabriel Zucman, using a comparable database as the earlier Saez-Zucman study referenced above, examined the distribution of national income in much the same way as the earlier study examined wealth.[80]

---

80 Thomas Piketty, Emmanuel Saez, and Gabriel Zucman, "Distribution of National Accounts: Methods and Estimates for the United States," *The Quarterly Journal of Economics* 133, no. 2 (May 2018): 553–609, doi:10. 1093/qie/qix043.

This work, entitled "Distribution of National Accounts: Methods and Estimates for the United States," includes a calculation of income on both a pretax and posttax bases. The posttax series deducts all taxes and adds back all government transfer payments, such as Social Security, Medicare, Medicaid, Earned Income Tax Credit, Aid to Families with Dependent Children, Food Stamps, and Supplemental Security Income. Also added back to individuals is an allocation of governmental indirect services, including education, police, and defense. This methodology provides far more complete information than had been previously available. Moreover, it enabled the authors, for the first time in studies of this nature, to determine the disposition of income by income group in a way that is consistent with total national income. Nothing is left out. It all ties together.

A second difference in this data when compared to other studies is that the authors corrected household income data to account for changing marital and cohabitation patterns by individualizing reported household income, which resulted in a greater number of income units.[81]

Finally, I would like to note that unlike all the previous tables in this book where the economic measure is *gross domestic product (GDP)*, in the Piketty, Saez, and Zucman analysis, it is *national income.* The difference between the two is that national income is GDP less capital depreciation plus net income received from abroad. Capital depreciation is a noncash charge, an accounting convention intended to recognize the cost of capital already incurred by amortizing it over time. It is typically equivalent to about 16% of GDP. Income received from abroad is the net of interest, dividends, and other receipts paid by foreign persons or entities less interest, dividends, and other receipts paid by US persons or entities to foreign persons or entities. It typically amounts to 2–4% of GDP.

On the following page are two tables that dissect the distribution of national income to the top income groups. These are presented as a test

---

81 Later in this book (chapter 12), we will examine income distribution using data compiled by the Congressional Budget Office based on Internal Revenue Service, Census Bureau, and Federal Reserve sources. This compilation differs from the Piketty, Saez, and Zucman database, but the trend lines are comparable.

of Milanovic's assertion that in recent decades, income is increasingly concentrated within a minority of the population. They illustrate such concentration within the hierarchy of income groups comprising the top 10%, and clearly confirm Milanovic's line of reasoning. Probably the most stunning example of extreme growth in concentration is that of the 23,440 adults, comprising the top 0.01%, whose 1984 average income of $6.1 million increased by $14.3 million to $20.4 million by 2014. Out of this $14.3 million increase in yearly income, $10.2 million came from a redistribution of income from the bottom 99%.

Here's another interesting fact: in terms of total national income, the top 10.0% increased their annual share by $893.8 billion, every penny of which came from the bottom 90.0%. Said differently, on average, for each year between 1984 and 2014, every one of the 211 million adults in the bottom 90% contributed $6,000 apiece to the welfare of the top 10%.

Table 9. Percent of National Income by Income Group

Income Group	Number of Adults 2014	Income per Adult after Tax and Transfer 1984	Income per Adult after Tax and Transfer 2014	% of National Income 1984	% of National Income 2014
Total Population	234,400,000	$42,458	$64,633	100.0%	**100.0%**
Bottom 90.0%	210,960,000	$31,536	$43,723	66.7%	**60.8%**
Top 10.0%	23,440,000	$140,757	$252,822	33.3%	**39.2%**
Top 1.0%	2,344,000	$458,824	$1,012,429	10.9%	**15.8%**
Top 0.1%	234,400	$1,674,849	$4,425,050	4.0%	**6.9%**
Top 0.01%	23,440	$6,081096	$20,337,563	1.5%	**3.1%**

Source: Piketty, Saez, and Zucman (2018), appendix, main data, *Average National Income, Fiscal Income, and CPS Income*, http://gabriel-zucman. eu/esdina.

Table 10. Attribution of Increased Income from Change in Share

Income Group	Increased Income per Adult 1984–2014	Amount from Economic Growth	Amount from Change in Share	% from Change in Share	Compound Annual Growth Rate of Change in Share
Total Population	$22,175	$22,175	0	0	-
Bottom 90.0%	$12,187	$17,244	$(5,996)	(49.2)%	(0.7)%
Top 10.0%	$112,066	$74,522	$37,543	33.5%	0.8%
Top 1.0%	$553,695	$241,803	$311,802	56.3%	1.7%
Top 0.1%	$2,750,201	$904,844	$1,845,357	67.1%	2.5%
Top 0.01%	$14,292467	$4,111,187	$10,181,280	71.2%	3.3%

Source: Piketty, Saez, and Zucman (2018), appendix, main data, *Average National Income, Fiscal Income, and CPS Income*, http://gabriel-zucman.eu/esdina.

From this discussion and the accompanying tables, it should be evident that Milanovic's findings regarding the escalation of income and wealth of the top income groups at the expense of the lower income groups is easily demonstrable. A related finding is that the income of the top groups is increasingly dominated by labor income as opposed to capital income. This idea is reinforced by anecdotal evidence when we think about the extraordinary compensation of corporate executives, Wall Street investment bankers, entertainers, rock stars, sports figures, and the like whose economic gains can provide substance to somewhat slim statistical data.

However, tax records going back as far as 1913 provide some help. In past years, most people comprising the upper strata did not go to work for a living like ordinary people. Rather, the top income groups were largely populated by people living off their capital, clipping coupons, and living on interest, dividends, and distributions from private entities.

Now, however, this group is giving way to those whose income comes from employment. One way to gauge this is to examine the income of the top 0.01% of the population. In 1975, this cohort comprised 14,630 people, who had income of approximately $3.3 million per year, which in the aggregate was $49.0 billion and represented 0.9% of national income. Yet by 2012, this group, now numbering twenty-three thousand people, had income averaging $20.0 million per year, which in the aggregate amounted to about $470.0 billion, or 3.2% of national income. As for the labor or wage component in the upper income groups, the data appears limited to the top 1.0%. In 1975, labor in the top 1.0% was 4.1% of national income, or $223 million. By 2012, the labor component had risen to 9.3%, or $1.4 billion.

Regarding wealth, the threshold for the top 0.01% in 2012 was approximately $111.0 million, and the average wealth of this group was about $371.0 million. However, the upper ranges of income and wealth are considerably higher because the top 0.01% also includes the 630 or so billionaires in the United States.

Perhaps a better way to visualize the growth of income and wealth, as well as the changing relationship between the two, is to examine the following chart, where the rate of increase in income since the mid-1980s is so strong that it is running ahead of the increase in wealth, which may suggest a break in the traditional relationship. However, if the past is any guide, we may be fairly certain that the accumulation of concentrated wealth will soon catch up as various forms of deferred compensation (such as stock options and nonqualified pension arrangements) are realized.

Figure 2. Income and Wealth: Top 0.1% 1915–2012

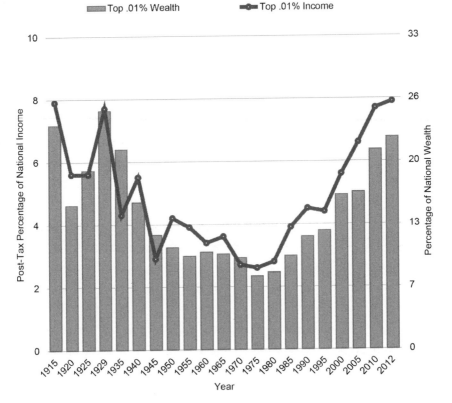

Sources: Saez and Zucman (2014), appendix, main data.
Piketty, Saez, and Zucman (2018), appendix, main data, table B1.

This chart, figure 2, illustrates the decline in both income and wealth experienced by the top 0.1% of the US population during the period 1929 through 1950. It then shows a thirty-five-year period (1950–1985) when this group's share of national wealth stabilized at around 10%. Following this lengthy period of stability, the share of the top 0.1% more than doubled during the next twenty-seven years. However, there almost appears to be an inverse relationship between wealth concentration and growth of per capita GDP, because in no period on this chart did growth in per capita GDP equal that of 1950–1985 when the distribution of income and wealth was in better balance than it is now. From this, I would infer that if inequalities act to suppress

CHARLES L. LADNER

growth and if there is historical precedent to correcting inequality, then there may be hope for the future. This matter will be taken up in chapters 12 and 13.

The core assumptions of liberal meritocratic capitalism are (1) the increasing concentration of income and wealth at the upper levels and (2) the increasing incidence of high-wealth people also being high-wage earners.

Another distinguishing element, and perhaps the most important of all, is the way in which the centrality of an increasing concentration of wealth is so predictably crystalized by the biological imperative that constitutes the overarching theme of this book. Recall that it is the primordial compulsion for survival and reproduction, otherwise summarized as selfishness (or, in the world of economics, greed), that compels all human behavior. Capitalism ideally suits this most primary human motivation. And loosely regulated capitalism, as we have experienced in the United States over the past forty years, is the perfect vehicle for its economic expression. Thus, the outcome, in the form of Milanovic's liberal meritocratic capitalism, is entirely predictable: given spectacular technology-led creative destruction in the Schumpeterian sense, it is almost inevitable that spectacular income and wealth inequality would follow.

Liberal meritocratic capitalism is certainly different from that that preceded it, but whether it represents a temporary anomaly of the English-speaking countries or is truly the wave of the future and whether it can avoid the internal inconsistencies of capitalism are questions to be addressed in the last chapter.

Now we must take up the matter of political capitalism, which Milanovic´ submits as the most likely rival to liberal meritocratic capitalism in the future.

CHAPTER ELEVEN

Types of Capitalism: Political Capitalism

J UST AS MILANOVIC´ singles out the United States as the archetype of liberal meritocratic capitalism, so, too, does he identify China as the archetype of political capitalism. However, China is not alone. He classifies ten other countries in this category, notably Vietnam, Malaysia, Singapore, Algeria, Angola, and a few others, primarily Sub-Saharan African countries. Moreover, he sees this as a wave of the future and expects many other less well-developed countries to follow China's example.

He finds that these economies have three systemic characteristics in common:

1. Efficient bureaucracy
2. Absence of the rule of law
3. Autonomy of the state. Decisions arbitrary, not bound by law.

China: The Archetype of Political Capitalism

When Deng Xiaoping made the decision to jettison socialism and replace it with free market capitalism in the late 1970s, he did so with a uniquely Chinese perspective. It was done in small stages and quietly, with the government always maintaining that such change was a natural evolution of socialism. Economic reform began in the rural areas with the privatization of agriculture, followed by the creation of township and village enterprises owned by local communities (TVEs). By the mid-1980s, virtually all Chinese agriculture was in private hands; and by the year 2000, the TVEs, employing upward of ninety-two million people, had been acquired by private entrepreneurs.[82] Meanwhile, in the urban areas, small privately owned shops began to spring up, and the state-owned enterprises (SOEs) began to falter such that in 1994, the newly enacted Company Law allowed the SOEs to convert to joint stock companies, providing the legal basis for their acquisition or control by private interests.[83]

The Chinese people, once liberated from the constraints of socialism, spontaneously grew their economy very fast—and with reckless abandon. The leadership, delighted on the one hand by the extraordinary wealth generated by their people and wary on the other hand of losing control, created an administrative structure to provide control at the periphery of the economy to prevent the business and entrepreneurial class from converting its economic power to political power. Interestingly, in this chaotic Wild West period of expansion, a close bond emerged between the controlling bureaucracy and private enterprise in the form of payoffs, embezzlement, and other unsavory forms of corruption, which were enabled by the absence of the sort of commercial and business laws common in Western capitalist states but unnecessary and therefore totally absent in socialist states.

The foundation on which capitalism rests is the free market that allocates resources and sets prices in response to market demand. Likewise, the foundation on which socialism rests is the administered market in which the allocation of resources and formulation of prices is carried out by governmental edict in response to central planning. Thus, free market pricing is the essential prerequisite of capitalism, and state-administered pricing is the essential prerequisite of socialism.

The following table sets forth the changes in China's pricing discipline from 1978 (the year of Mao's death) to 1999. It provides a

---

82 James A. Dorn, *The Genesis and Evolution of China's Economic Liberalization,* Cato Working Paper no. 38 (Washington, DC: CATO Institute, 2016), 10–13, accessed May 29, 2020, www.cato.org/working/papers.
83 Ibid., 25.

simple yet incontrovertible guide to both the rate and degree of China's economic transformation.

Table 11. Share of Transactions Conducted at Market Prices

	1978	1985	1991	1995	1999
Producer Goods					
Market Prices	**0%**	**13%**	**46%**	**78%**	**86%**
State Guided	0%	23%	18%	6%	4%
State Fixed	100%	64%	36%	16%	10%
Retail Sales					
Market Prices	**3%**	**34%**	**69%**	**89%**	**95%**
State Guided	0%	19%	10%	2%	1%
State Fixed	97%	47%	21%	9%	4%
Farm Commodities					
Market Prices	**6%**	**40%**	**58%**	**79%**	**83%**
State Guided	2%	23%	20%	4%	7%
State Fixed	93%	37%	22%	17%	9%

Source: Dorn (2016), 29.

This table was compiled by James A. Dorn, with data originally assembled by the OECD. It is quite revealing, for it shows that in the relatively short time span of twenty years, virtually all pricing of goods and services in the Chinese economy moved from state control to market control. And thus, over a mere twenty years, the entirety of China's economic machinery was transformed from socialism, where the state sets prices, to capitalism, where the market sets prices.

Milanovic' will tell us that this transition came with strings attached. The state or, more precisely, the Chinese Communist Party (CCP) officials charged with overseeing the economy had considerable latitude in interpreting and applying the nation's porous web of poorly developed commercial laws. In practice, this meant that their rulings were, more often than not, favorable to private interests so long as they themselves personally benefitted. Thus was born a symbiotic culture of corruption that, to the present day, dominates the Chinese economy from the periphery to the center and that creates a community of interest between businessmen and administrators. In China, the elites, both political and capitalist, are as one. And according to Milanovic´, it was this relationship that provided the catalyst to China's phenomenal growth during the thirty years following the death of Mao.

However, with the ascendency of Xi Jinping in 2012, a member of the Communist Party aristocracy from birth, Beijing began to signal a more restrictive and puritanical attitude toward the control of society. The first sign of this was the initiation of an anti-corruption campaign. It is claimed that over one million people were caught up in this net, including some very high-ranking party members whose fraudulent spoils were indeed extraordinary. Some of the abuses, though evidently quite common, are hard to believe. To get a flavor for these goings-on, Milanavic´ provides the following anecdotes:

> Xu Caihu, at the time of his arrest in 2014 the vice chairman of the Central Military Commission and the highest official to be indicted to that date, had the entire basement of his 20,000-square foot house stacked with cash (renminbi's, euros and dollars) that weighed more than a ton. The precious artifacts filled ten military trucks. The largest seizure of cash since the founding of the People's Republic concerned a deputy head of the coal department in the National Energy Administration who was found with more than 200 million yuan in cash (about $26 million at the current exchange rate). Sixteen machines-counting machines were brought in; four burned out in the process of counting the bills ... The list goes on.

While more than one million people have been caught up in this dragnet, it is believed that this number is but the tip of the iceberg; and though the anti-corruption campaign is still in process, it should be remembered that with a population of 1.4 billion and a party membership of 90.0 million, it is unlikely that the program will do little more than modestly contain the problem. Moreover, one must wonder whether the party leadership is truly serious about dealing with the problem, because all indications point to the fact that China's leadership had clearly seen that a corrupt economy functioning independent of direct political control has unexpected advantages—first, in supplying supplemental compensation to the CCP political elite and second, in insulating the leadership from the political risk of unequal distribution of resources and income. Moreover, the CCP being an autonomous political order controlling all the military and political machinery, allowing the creation of a class of independently wealthy party officials side by side with the equally independent capitalist class, offers little or no political risk because Xi and his cohort can always tighten the reins to protect themselves from any potential devolution of power. In a broader sense, we saw this response with the Tiananmen Square massacre and the current clampdown in Hong Kong. We also see this in the heightened intensity of Maoist-like restrictions on the general population currently surfacing under Xi's leadership.

However, notwithstanding its independent political stature as the sole instrument of government control and its intake of the spoils of corruption, the Chinese Communist Party (CCP) continues to be insecure in its relationship with the dynamic new capitalist interests embedded within their country. Consequently, no sooner was Xi Jinping elected general secretary of the CCP and effectively sole leader of the nation (later confirmed by his being elected president of China by the National People's Congress) than the party, inspired and led by Xi, embarked on the aggressive anti-corruption campaign, ostensibly to purify the party but in reality to purge all possible rivals, notably those in a position to challenge his rule. A side benefit has been to curb the excesses that may be seen to seduce key party (and thus, government)

CHARLES L. LADNER

officials, diluting their loyalty to the CCP and, by extension, the autonomy of the Xi clique.

It has been said regarding communism that "once you strip away socialism, you're left with fascism." Well, that may be true; but in the case of China, it was not instantaneous. Even though socialism disappeared by the early 1990s, the Communist Party still claimed to be the champions of socialism (although the facts on the ground argued otherwise). Yet if socialism evaporated during the 1980s, how did the CCP avoid the descent into fascism for thirty years?

In response, I would suggest that the party leadership who succeeded Mao and his Gang of Four had been so traumatized by Mao's aberrant cruelty that after his death, they were determined to avoid the risk of one-man rule in the future. To that end, they constructed an oligarchic party and governmental structure that dispersed authority among a group of individuals. During this period (1978–1992), Deng Xiaoping, who never held the top leadership position but was so influential that he may best be described as the first among equals, emerged as the public face of China—its paramount leader.

Deng retired in 1992. Others followed, but they were always functioning within the oligarchic structure, until the ascendancy of Xi Jinping in 2012. Now with memories of Mao's irrational tyranny beginning to fade, the implicit authoritarian bias of communism began to surface in the behavior of Xi.

Xi's sense of entitlement, faithfulness to the CCP aristocracy of which he was a member by birth, and his absolutist tendencies and ideological rigidity stand in sharp contrast to Deng, under whose leadership the concept of political capitalism evolved. Early in the period of transition from socialism to capitalism, Deng and others in the leadership justified their seeming apostasy from pure socialist doctrine by describing their policies as being "socialism with Chinese characteristics." They described it as like a bird in a cage, with the bird being the private sector and the cage being the state. Make the cage too small and the economy will be stifled. Make it large and expansive and the economy will have the freedom to grow. Make it too large and the state is threatened. Clearly, during the 1990s and subsequent decades,

China's leadership got it right. The economy, as we all know, flourished beyond anyone's imagination.

But for the CCP, it's a question of balance. How large to make the cage? Ultimately, that is a subjective judgment, which has been largely in the hands of Xi Jinping since 2012; and with Xi, the cage is slowly and inexorably diminishing.

Concurrent with his ascendency in 2012, Xi initiated a political purge under the guise of the anti-corruption campaign, which appears to be continuing to this day. This provided Xi with the opportunity to take charge of most of the party and government leadership positions vacated by censured high-level party officials. At the same time, he established under his personal supervision a number of supragovernmental commissions to oversee large elements of society. Such consolidation of power was followed by the incorporation of the thought of Xi Jinping into the constitution and the subsequent rise of a cult of personality. All this consolidation of political power culminated in the party-controlled National People's Congress removal of presidential term limits in 2018, thus assuring Xi's unchallenged leadership for life—a distinction that had been accorded only to Mao in the past.

Early in his tenure, Xi implemented severe censorship over both public and journalistic discussion of such topics as constitutional democracy, promarket neoliberalism, media independence, universal values (those that might transcend China's political values), criticism of past practices, and finding fault with the nature of Chinese-style socialism. Then in logical progression, the government began to impose increased control over the internet to reinforce this newly invigorated climate of censorship. Under Xi's concept of internet sovereignty, Google and Facebook have been censured. Weibo, the Chinese version of Twitter, has been all but disabled by the imposition of criminal penalties, including imprisonment for posts that violate the censor's interpretations of what is allowed. And as of April 2019, Wikipedia has been completely blocked. Moreover, the government, with the aid of private industry, has developed a sophisticated technology known as the

Great Firewall that currently employs upward of two million people to monitor all internet content flowing throughout China.[84]

Suppression of free speech, while definitely the rule in earlier years, was less common in the years following the death of Mao. But now with the ascendency of Xi, many of the old Maoist practices are being reinstated. One conspicuously problematic scheme is the acceleration of intense personal surveillance accommodated by the installation of a nationwide system of video cameras. These cameras are now augmented by advanced facial recognition technology. Currently, there are approximately two hundred million such cameras in use in China, with an expectation that this number will increase to over three hundred million by 2021. However, there's more to this invasive policy. The nation's pervasive surveillance technology, as dystopian as it may seem, is now being combined in an even more oppressive form by its use to support China's social credit system.[85]

The social credit system is a massive data collection program designed to stockpile detailed information about the behavior of every Chinese citizen, evaluate their trustworthiness, and provide penalties for behavior deemed unacceptable.[86] The system itself still remains differentiated and fragmented by geographic jurisdiction, but the government is moving quickly to enforce uniformity to meet its expressed goal of universal application to all of the nation's 1.4 billion people. While originally aimed at fraudulent or criminal activities, ordinary citizens are now evaluated on such things as how polite they are to their neighbors, whether they properly care for their parents, or whether they are prompt in paying their bills and credit card charges. It is a point system, and

---

84 Elizabeth C. Economy, "The Great Firewall of China: Xi Jinping's Internet Shutdown," *The Guardian* (June 29, 2018), accessed, June 22, 2020, www.theguardian.com/news/2018/jun/2018/the-great-firewall-of-china-xi-jimping's-internet-shutdown.

85 Simina Mistreamu, "Life within China's Social Credit Laboratory," *Foreign Policy* (April 3, 2018), accessed June 23, 2020, www.foreignpolicy.com/04/03/2018/life/within/china's/social/ctrdit/laboratory.

86 Thomas Piketty, *Capital and Ideology*, trans. Arthur Goldhammer (Cambridge: The Belknap Press of Harvard University Press, 2020), 619.

if one's points are too low, that person can be blacklisted from such privileges as buying airline tickets or traveling on high-speed trains. According to the *South China Morning Post* in February 2019, "17.5 million people were restricted from buying plane tickets and 5.5 million were restricted from purchasing high-speed train tickets,"[87] and yet the system isn't even fully rolled out. Of course, penalties for serious transgressions are referred to the courts and criminal justice system. It is thus apparent that Xi's intention, by means of the nation's unthinkably intrusive electronic surveillance and its suffocating social credit system, is to bring the whole population under the full control of a CCP-organized police state.

In the relatively short time Xi has been in office, he has made notable progress in concentrating political power in his own hands and in restoring the strongman rule so closely identified with Mao and China's historic past. Moreover, at the same time, through the mechanism of the electronic surveillance and social credit systems, he has outdone his predecessors by successfully bringing the population to heel with an efficiency and effectiveness they never could have imagined. In addition, Xi has already exceeded whatever imperial ambitions the Mao generation might have entertained by moving beyond China's borders and initiating a sophisticated imperialistic policy through the Belt and Road program of infrastructure construction and financing provided by China's engineering firms and its banks.

All this rapid change and frenetic activity raises questions regarding China's economic future. Since Xi has now positioned himself as China's new Mao, what are his motivations? For it would seem that whatever drives Xi will drive China. And secondly, where is Xi taking China? Is he taking China forward to a glorious future, or is he leading backward toward the self-destructive ruination of the Mao years?

---

87   He Huifeng, "How Does China's Social Credit System Work?" *South China Morning Post* (February 18, 2019), accessed June 24, 2020, https://scmp.com/news/china/society/article/2186606/chinas-social-credit-system-shows-its-teeth-banning-millions.

Who Is Xi Jinping?

Firstly, to address questions about Xi's motivating principles, I will refer to a US Department of State report prepared in 2009 for Jon Huntsman Jr. who was then the United States ambassador to China. The document is now in the public record and was originally intended to provide background material regarding Xi Jinping, who at that time was seemingly the apparent heir to China's then president, Hu Jintao. See below:

> Xi is a true "elitist" at heart … believing that rule by a dedicated and committed communist party leadership is the key to enduring social stability and national strength. The most permanent influences shaping Xi's worldview were his "princeling" pedigree and formative years growing up with families of first-generation CCP revolutionaries in Beijing's exclusive residential compounds … Xi has a genuine sense of "entitlement", believing that members of his generation are "legitimate heirs" to the revolutionary achievements of their parents and therefore "deserve to rule China."[88]

Born in 1953, Xi lived a life of privilege for most of his youth. But in 1963, his father was purged and sent to work managing a rural factory. In 1966, when Xi was thirteen, the Cultural Revolution cut short his education. Two years later, his father was imprisoned. The family was persecuted and lost its benefits, and Xi was sent to the countryside. During this period, his sister was killed in a home invasion by revolutionaries, and it is believed his mother was forced to commit suicide. The good life was truly finished for Xi Jinping.

In 1975, his father was released from prison (fully rehabilitated by the party in 1978). In that same year, 1975, at the age of twenty-two,

---

88 "Portrait of Vice-President Xi Jinping: 'Ambitious Survivor' of the Cultural Revolution" (November 16, 2009), accessed June 20, 2020, http://wikileaks.org/plusd/cables/09beijing3128a_html.

Xi entered Tsinghua University as a worker-peasant-soldier student. He had earlier (1974) been allowed to enter the Communist Party, and according to the US State Department, it was at that point in his life that he resolved to become "redder than the red." Now after having received his degree in 1979 and with his father finally restored to good graces in the Communist Party and again elevated to leadership, Xi embarked on a political party career that over the following thirty-seven years of loyal and diligent service brought him to the pinnacle of party and national leadership.

Xi is the most important leader since Mao, and his thought, like that of Mao, is now enshrined in China's constitution. In 2018, the *New York Times* published a summary of this voluminous body of work.[89] Reduced to three main points, Xi's doctrine first calls for the restoration of China to the glories and military/political hegemony of past dynasties like the Han, Ming, and early Qing. Having inherited a flourishing economy that is on its way to world domination or, at a minimum, an equal sharing of world domination with the United States, he is now engaged in broadening and strengthening the military and may soon cause it to advance beyond the United States as the most powerful in the world. Consistent with its impressive economy and strong military, China is now asserting itself on the world stage. The massive Belt and Road initiative, which is much less benign than would seem from first appearances, is now emerging as a vehicle for China's territorial aspirations. At the same time, the advancement into the South China Sea, the coming takeover of Hong Kong, and the threats to Taiwan are all predictive symptoms of China's new and aggressive assertiveness.

The second pillar of the Xi doctrine is to strengthen the Communist Party to a position where it's primacy within China can never be challenged. This means not only repairing internal party discipline by such means as the anti-corruption campaign but also bringing the entire population under its thumb. For Xi, this is critical. He brooks no ambiguity on this point, hence the astounding level of electronic

---

89 Chris Buckley, "Xi Doctrine Will Guide a Nation," *New York Times*, February 27, 2018, section A, page 8, New York edition.

CHARLES L. LADNER

surveillance extended to every single citizen all the time and everywhere without relief; plus an all-enveloping personal record system incarnated in the mechanism of the Social Credit organization, which is the most intrusive and intensely personal tracking of individual behavior ever devised by humankind.

Finally, the third pillar of the Xi doctrine is Xi himself. To all outward appearances, he is postured as a visionary idealist; and by his actions, it is clear that he views himself as an indispensable leader. Yet as evidenced by the pattern of his career, it is clear that his quest for supremacy has been consistently motivated not by reasons of ego engrossment or personal gain but rather, as noted in the US State Department report, by his sense of entitlement and his deeply held beliefs that only he and his fellow princelings have the requisite perspective and moral standing to guide the nation to the triumph for which it is destined. Thus, he has portrayed himself as finding it necessary to assume all the most important party, military, and political leadership positions while assuring the perpetuity of his rule and the constitutional enshrinement of his ideals—and then capping it all by a nationwide cult of personality. China is a vast and disparate place, and its historical weakness has been its people's fractious and discordant interests, so Xi's recognition of the need for a single-party rule directed by a single strong leader is indisputably the most rational solution toward achieving the national unity that is the prerequisite to China once again ascending to glory. And in the end, it is China's ascension to glory that is Xi's dream. So who is Xi Jinping?

It seems fairly obvious that he is a disinterested idealist. It also is obvious that he has an obsessive hunger for power. And considered in that light, one must ask whether there are historical parallels, perhaps from the not-too-distant past? Clearly it is not Mao. Mao Zedong was an ideologue (with a trace of insanity), and Xi is far too pragmatic and far too sane to ever be grouped with the likes of Mao. On the other hand, with Chinese characteristics, could he be the reincarnation of one such as Mussolini? This may sound bizarre, but wittingly or not, Xi is rapidly creating a fascist state. All the signs point to this. The sanctification of Xi as the wise and decisive leader, his personal monopolization of all critical party and political positions, the insistence on a one-party body politics, the imposition of absolute control of the population, the creation of pervasive police state disciplines, the needless buildup of the military (needless for a nation with no external enemies), the economic incursions into smaller states, the all-too-credible threat of overseas military expansion, and the ubiquitous promotion of national pride—all these things are the indisputable marks of fascism.

Where Is Xi Jinping and the Communist Party Taking China?

The only part of Chinese society that could realistically mitigate the nation's unmistakable procession toward fascism is its vigorous and somewhat independent private economic sector. Milanovic´ is clear on this matter when he writes this: "The viability of political capitalism as a successful model rests on (1) the ability to insulate politics from economic, which is intrinsically difficult because the state plays such an important role, and (2) the ability to maintain a relatively uncorrupt 'backbone' that can enforce decisions that are in the national interest, not just the narrow business interest."[90]

Milanovic's opinion refers mainly to the probability of China exporting its brand of capitalism or serving as a model for others to copy. I will argue, on the other hand, that in light of fundamental biological tensions, Milanovic's analysis applies even more coherently to the viability and endurance of the political capitalism *within* China than the export of the system *outside* the country, because if the theory of political capitalism fails to endure within China, it will hardly be a model for others to replicate.

The biological tensions are the overarching theme of this work, and it's summarized as follows:

Every living thing, as discussed elsewhere in this book, is possessed of the instinct for survival and reproduction as its first order of activity.

---

90 Milanovic (2019), 128.

This instinct may be capsulized by the term *selfishness*, or *self-interest*. In all living organisms, the compulsion of selfishness is the biological precedent to everything the organism does. It is the foundation on which all activity is carried out. Frustrating an organism's inherent selfishness by preventing its realization will cause the death of the organism or its incapacity to immortalize its genes. Either outcome is incompatible with the principle of life itself.

No organism will freely allow this to happen. Confronted with any impediment or barrier to the organism's selfish drive, the organism will respond with either a direct and frequently violent challenge or it will search for alternative means to achieve satisfaction. This is the biological tension that affects all aspects of economic behavior. Translating these fundamentals into the language of human behavior and, more specifically, the language of economics is not difficult.

Economists have long portrayed capitalism as being driven by enlightened self-interest.[91] And as detailed in chapters 8 and 9, humankind has never devised a system as effective as capitalism for the production and distribution of material wealth. Owing to the spread of capitalism throughout the world, more people have more wealth than ever before in history. Yet we also know that capitalism can be the source of the most cruel and extreme forms of economic injustice, often expressed by racism, human bondage, and poverty in the midst of prosperity. Thus, it is in capitalism, for good or for bad, that we see the biological compulsion of selfishness fully embodied in social behavior.

The antithesis of capitalism is socialism. It, too, responds to the biological requirements of selfishness. As discussed in chapters 4 through 6, socialism is a system built on the denial of this most human characteristic—a denial of the instinct for survival and reproduction, without which even life itself would fail to exist. And in every instance where socialism has been tried, its attenuation of human instinctive selfishness seems to always result in social and political collapse.

---

91 I am not so sure about the *enlightened* part, but I am absolutely certain about the *self-interest* part.

Yet notwithstanding these commonly known facts, China's president, Xi Jinping, and his Communist Party companions persist in the adherence to this ideology. Early in 2019, the party's intellectual journal, *Qiushi*, published a speech by Xi addressed to the party's central committee on the subject of socialism with Chinese characteristics. This is Xi Jinping on socialism:[92]

> First of all: *Socialism with Chinese Characteristics is socialism.* It is not any other sort of "ism." The foundational scientific principles of socialism cannot be abandoned; only if they are abandoned would our system no longer be socialist. From first to last our Party has emphasized that "socialism with Chinese Characteristics" adheres to the basic principles of scientific socialism and is imbued with characteristically Chinese features bestowed by the conditions of the times. Socialism with Chinese characteristics is socialism, not any other "ism."
>
> In recent years there have been a few commentators—both at home and abroad—that have asked if what modern China is doing can really be socialism. Some have said that we have engaged in a sort of "capital socialism" or "bureaucratic capitalism." *These labels are completely wrong.* We say that socialism with Chinese characteristics is socialism. No matter how we reform and open up, we should always adhere to the socialist road with Chinese characteristics, the theoretical systems of socialism with Chinese characteristics, the structure of socialism with Chinese characteristics, and the basic requirements put forward by the Eighteenth National Congress of the Communist Party of China for a new victory of socialism. These include: the absolute leadership of the Communist Party of China,

---

92 Tanner Greer, "Xi Jinping in Translation: China's Guiding Ideology," *Palladium Magazine* (May 31, 2019), accessed June 6, 2020, paladiummag.com/2019/05/31/xi-jinping-in-translation-chinas-guiding-ideology/.

CHARLES L. LADNER

grounding policy in national conditions, putting economic construction at the center, adhering to the "Four Cardinal Principles" (The Four Cardinal Principles are: 1) Adhering to the socialist path, 2) the people's democratic dictatorship, 3) the supreme leadership of the Communist Party of China, and 4) Marxist-Leninism and Mao-Zedong Thought), and to the program of reform and opening up, liberating and developing productive social forces, building a socialist market economy, socialist democratic politics, an advanced socialist culture, a harmonious socialist society, and an ecological socialist civilization.

As a matter of first impression, this is an astounding document. While these are only the opening paragraphs, the entire speech is laced with references to China of today as a socialist economy. Yet we can be reasonably certain that Xi and his advisers are well informed of the current situation, so it seems preposterous that he should be so insistent on China's socialism (even if it comes with Chinese characteristics).

Here are the facts: The share of 2017 GDP contributed by the public sector state-owned enterprises (SOEs) was estimated by the World Bank to be a maximum of 28%. Thus, 72% of 2017 GDP was contributed by the private sector, while at the same time, the SOEs' share of 2017 employment was a maximum of 16%, and the private sector's was 84%.[93] Moreover, when it comes to the free market, as noted in table 11 in chapter 10, by 1999, the market determined the prices and allocation

---

93   The World Bank analysts rely on data provided by China's National Bureau of Statistics and other less-than-fully-credible sources. Accordingly, they note that because the data is incomplete and not straightforward, they construct estimates based on partial information. See Chunlin Zhung, "How Much Do State-Owned Enterprises Contribute to China's GDP and Employment?" World Bank (July 15, 2019), accessed July 6, 2020, document1.Worldbank.org/curated/en/449701565248091726/pdf/how-much-do-state-owned-enterprises-contribute-to-china-s-gdp-and-employment.pdf.

for 86% of producer goods, 95% of retail goods, and 83% of farm commodities. Is this data, in any possible way, consistent with socialism?

Of course not! Xi appears to be using the socialist tag in much the same way as autocrats of the past have done. They do it in a ludicrous effort to put a gloss on their despotic realities. Remember that Hitler's Nazi Party was the National *Socialist* Party, Ulbricht's East Germany was the German *Democratic* Republic, and Stalin's Russia was the Union of Soviet Socialist *Republics*.

Today's China is no more socialist than the United States. But perhaps Xi is not really describing China as it is today but rather China as he expects it to be. Perhaps his expressed doctrine is aspirational.

Given the conditions on the ground—the undeniable capitalist character of the economy and the resolute momentum toward fascism—combined with Xi's aspiration, it is perfectly clear that Xi is taking China along the path of socialism. And the further China travels this road, the closer it will get to the same outcomes socialism always delivers, namely, economic stagnation and failure. This will not happen overnight, but Xi is now sixty-seven years old; his internal clock probably gives him about twenty years. So it is reasonable to expect an economic slowdown within that time frame for exactly the same reasons as it occurred in the Soviet Union.

Furthermore, it is a distinct possibility that the process could be accelerated. Political scholar Dr. Minxin Pei, writing in *Foreign Affairs*, suggests that China's growth will be impaired by, among other things, the combination of ballooning debt, an aging population, and the policy of the United States to reduce its dependence on Chinese imports. Moreover, China's governance structure, which during the period of its greatest growth was a collective leadership, has now (since 2012) been replaced by the rule of an autocratic strongman. And the problem that Pei sees with this is the difficulty of correcting policy mistakes because for Xi to admit error and reverse policy decisions would undercut the image of infallibility, which is essential to sustaining the legitimacy of

CHARLES L. LADNER

his rule.[94] Thus, the political flexibility to sustain free market capitalism will be lost as a victim of political sclerosis.

Ming also points to the decoupling of the US and Chinese economies whereby the United States (as well as other nations) will substantially reduce its dependence on imports from China, resulting in a net negative impact on the Chinese economy. Geopolitician George Friedman is even more convinced of this vulnerability:

> The most important thing to understand about China is that its domestic market cannot financially absorb the product of its industrial plant. Yes, China has grown, but its growth has made it hostage to its foreign customers. Nearly 20 percent of China's gross domestic product is generated from exports … anything that could reduce China's economy for the long term by about 20 percent is a desperate vulnerability.[95]

Therefore, I would conclude that the risks to the validity of political capitalism of failing to insulate economics from politics, as anticipated by Milanovic, are, in fact, in the early stages of realization. And judging from Xi's words and actions, it is only a matter of time before political capitalism is dismantled and replaced by full-scale socialism. It thus appears that Xi is trying to return to the world of Mao and the aristocratic bubble in which he was raised, and as in the past, this would be much to the advantage of the Communist Party elites but much to the disadvantage of the Chinese people.

---

94 Minxin Pei, "China's Coming Upheaval: Competition, the Coronavirus, and the Weakness of Xi Jinping," *Foreign Affairs* 99, no. 3 (May/June 2020): 82–95.
95 George Friedman, "The Truth about the US-China Thucydides Trap," *Geopolitical Futures* (July 14, 2020).

CHAPTER TWELVE

Wither Capitalism: Can It Continue as the Sole Source of Prosperity, or Will It Capitulate to Its Own Self-Destructive Tendencies?

I N THIS BOOK, I have tried to present an analysis of two economic systems—socialism and capitalism—from the perspective of evolution. Specifically, I have tried to present an analysis from the perspective of the evolutionary instruments of natural selection. which are the instincts of survival and reproduction. I then collapsed these two instincts into a single term: *selfishness.*

Selfishness is the primal instinct in humans. But beyond that, it is the unique quality that is essential not just to humans but to the growth and existence of all living things. Absent selfishness, there is no possibility of life. Selfishness is what distinguishes life from nonlife.

In the world of economics, it should seem obvious that a system that does not interfere with biological compulsion of selfishness has a higher probability of success than one that does interfere with it. Capitalism does not interfere with selfishness; in fact, it thrives on it. Socialism, on the other hand, is a contrived system that not only ignores the principles of natural selection but also actively cultivates its suppression. There is no moral judgment here. This is simply a statement of fact.

Socialism, as defined by Marx and Engels, as well as by every other theorist and practitioner, requires the support of a coercive governmental structure to function. Socialism and autocracy are always coextensive, because over time, people cannot freely submit to the disciplines that socialism demands. And in demanding uniform obedience from all its subjects, it acts to suppress each individual's embedded need of selfishness. There is no room for differences in opinion or economic interests. Socialism is a transactional construct that manifests the highest of ideals (and that is its attraction). It promises universal benefits for all in exchange for universal obedience by all.[96]

Earlier in this book, we discussed the inherent conflict between the disciplined uniformity required of people living under a socialist system and the involuntary pressure inherent in each such person to physically express his/her instinct of selfishness. The frustration of this instinct, which was clearly demonstrated in the case of the Soviet Union, resulted in a slow, almost imperceptible degradation of congregate economic behaviors. Again, in the case of the Soviet Union, after decades of apparently good economic performance, by the early 1970s, the compounding effects of denied selfishness began to appear with devastating impact: alcoholism rose to near epidemic proportions, absenteeism was commonplace, productivity fell to levels not seen since the czarist times, and the quality of manufactured goods fell so far as to be unsaleable in all but domestic markets where consumers had no choice.

But there's more ... Not only was there an impairment of each worker's potential to express his/her own unique quality of selfishness, which corroded the system from within, but also, of equal importance, the Soviet society itself was unable to naturally adapt to changes in the

---

96 This is not to say that socialization of important consumer needs—such as transportation, gas, water and electric service, employment security, health care, and other similar services—cannot fit nicely within a capitalist economy, and perhaps they are better done by the state than by private enterprise. But on the other hand, it is to say most emphatically that government ownership or control of the driving forces and source of commercial innovation within an economy, which is its dominant private sector, as occurs in socialist states, will inevitably lead to the decline in the standard of living and an increase of poverty for all the reasons enumerated in the preceding chapters.

worldwide economic environment as it should have done in conformity to the imperatives of natural selection at the group or societal level. What I mean to say is that the pairing of the socialist ideology with an authoritarian rule, without which socialism cannot exist, produces such extreme rigidity in governmental policy that it paralyzes the political order and thereby prevents its requisite adaptations. In Russia, there was no permitted variance from the dogma of Marx and Lenin; and from the 1917 Revolution onward, there arose a missionary zeal to propagate strict Marxist/Leninist communism as the heart of a new socialist international order radiating from its perfect apotheosis: Soviet Russia.

From 1917 through the 1980s, all good and true communists were inspired in thought and action by this evangelical fervor. Accordingly, when Russia achieved hegemony in Eastern Europe in the 1940s and as it successfully spread the gospel of communism throughout newly liberated former European colonies in Africa and Asia in the 1950s and '60s, it energetically proceeded to underwrite the financial deficiencies of these newly established regimes not simply to create a client state dependency but also, more importantly, to support their adoption of the communist doctrine and their full membership in the Communist International. Unfortunately for Russia, as time passed and as its economy began to crumble in the 1980s, the weight of providing such financial support became unsustainable; and by 1990, the negative leverage of this fixed burden became so punitive that it represented a principal factor causing the Soviet Union's total economic implosion. Decades earlier, the Soviets knew they had a problem, but the ideological rigidity of the old Stalinists prevented any realistic possibility of adaptation to changed circumstances. Moreover, when it was obvious to all that their economy needed a strong market or free enterprise input, the supreme autocratic leadership once again, solely for ideological reasons, resisted the demands of adaptation because they believed it to be unthinkably heretical. The Old Guard, the disciples of Stalin and the true believers of Marx and Lenin, had such blind faith that they ignored the realities on the ground, for to do otherwise and loosen the strictures of Marxist theory in order to survive (in a more or less Darwinian fashion) would mean their abandoning the faith on which they had built their lives

CHARLES L. LADNER

and thus acknowledging its inconsistency with the essence of what it is to be a human.

China, on the other hand, following the lead of the evolutionary instinct two years after the 1976 death of Mao, slowly abandoned socialism and took up a form of capitalism more compatible with their humanity. This was possible only because the ideologue (i.e., Mao) was no longer in command. Ten years later, a then humiliated Russia followed suit when economic collapse forced their hand.

The point behind this is that multilevel selection at the societal level was not possible so long as the countries adhered to the rigidity of socialism, an artificial construct that acted to frustrate the operation of natural selection at both the individual and group level. During the later period of socialist ascendancy, the people suffered by their society's inability to adapt to the ever-changing environment—an outcome that any evolutionary biologist easily could have predicted.

So as history has illustrated, socialism is always doomed to failure, and this is because it was deliberately designed to be a system contrary to the evolutionary mechanics of life.

But what about capitalism? If socialism is a failed project because it suppresses the machinery of nature, then would not capitalism, which works with nature, be destined to always succeed? The answer no! No, because capitalism contains within itself contradictions that if not controlled will distort nature and cause it to fail as ignominiously as socialism.

The Inherent Contradictions of Capitalism

In the United States and Great Britain during the late 1970s, the economy was burdened by effects of an exceedingly high rate of inflation coupled with a marked slowing of the rate of growth. Commonly called stagflation, the impact of this unpleasant phenomenon was especially damaging to the middle and lower classes, as wages lagged the rate of inflation and slow growth meant fewer jobs, rising unemployment, and even fewer opportunities for career advancement. The top 20%, as usual, had sufficient resources to weather the storm, although their accumulated wealth was eroded by exceedingly poor stock market performance coupled with an inflationary-induced reduction in the value of their investments, the combination of which reduced their purchasing power by the end of the 1970s by as much as 33%, even after giving full effect to the investment returns for the period.[97]

Since the late 1940s, people had become accustomed to an average annual rate of inflation, measured by changes in the consumer price index (CPI) of about 2.5%. But then suddenly in 1974, it soared to 12.2% —largely caused by the creation of OPEC and its increases in petroleum prices, which filtered down throughout the entire economy. Inflation remained high for the next several years, running between 4.8% and 9.0%, until 1979 when it again spiked, this time to 14.8%, followed by 12.4% in 1980.[98] The future did not look good for the United States. People wondered, *Can we even slide back into the darkness of the 1930s? Is capitalism destined to always fail?*

Thus was established the foundation of the Reagan-Thatcher revolution of the 1980s, which, in time, spawned the disease of hypercapitalism that has been contaminating the world's economy at an accelerating pace during the early decades of the present century. The descriptive terms *infection* and *contamination* are admittedly very strong and perhaps unfair descriptions of today's version of capitalism. To clarify my meaning, they are not intended to attribute motivation or intent to we who are as active participants to today's markets, but rather they are descriptive of the unwitting consequences of our actions. Indeed, as I will show, continuation on this present course will, in all probability, lead to the crash of our current economic system.

But first, before getting on to the main point, let us momentarily step back and recall that the notion that capitalism has within it the

97 The data regarding the S&P 500 for the period 1970–1980 is drawn from Macrotrends at www.macrotrends.net/2324/sp500-historical-chart-data, accessed July 26, 2021.

98 Alan S. Blinder, "The Anatomy of Double-Digit Inflation in the 1970's," in *Inflation: Causes and Effects*, ed. Robert E. Hall (Chicago: University of Chicago Press, 1982), 261–282.

seeds of its own destruction is not new. In fact, Marx and Engels constructed their whole theory of communism on the dialectical expectation that capitalism would self-destruct and be replaced by socialism. Unfortunately for the Marxists, it never happened, and it won't happen in the future as he described because they built their model on the naive precepts of extrapolation. They believed they discerned a pattern. The trends of the past and even the trend line of their own day could be simply extended into the future. For example, they observed in the world of Europe and England a seemingly never-ending investment in manufacturing plants. They assumed that this trend would proceed far beyond the stage where consumers could absorb the output of the plants. When this occurred, profits would diminish, losses would pile up, and factory owners would cut wages to below subsistence levels, all this causing the workers to rise up, revolutionize society, and create a socialist world. This was only one of Marx's many fantasies, all of which were grounded in the naive belief that human intervention was unimaginable, because in the logic of Marxism, extrapolating from current history, humans are assumed to behave like unreasoning, deterministic machines.

The use of extrapolative reasoning is very common. For example, people look at their retirement portfolio and see that it has gone up for the last year, so they extrapolate the past into the future, making spending decisions based solely on the expectation that what happened in the past will surely happen in the future. Of course, in real life, that rarely occurs.

And then there's always the curious example Paul Ehrlich, the Stanford University professor who, in 1968, published a book titled *The Population Bomb*, a neo-Malthusian screed that extrapolated trends in population growth to predict that the world's population would shortly and inevitably outrun its assumed fixed capacity to produce food supply. There was a lot of panic in the 1960s and 1970s about this, especially because it predicted that within the decade of the 1970s, hundreds of millions were certain to die of starvation. However, Ehrlich failed to reckon with human intervention in the person of Norman Borlaug, who, with teams of academic agronomists, created the Green Revolution that revolutionized agronomy and increased crop yields and food supply by an order of magnitude. The world's population did grow from three billion to seven billion as Ehrlich had predicted, but never has there been a shortage of food resources—once again demonstrating that predictions about the future based on extrapolations will always be incorrect unless human intervention, for good or for bad, is taken into consideration.

The analysis that follows is different. It is not an extrapolation. It is grounded on an understanding of how natural instincts determine behavior and how the unchecked expression of such instincts can lead to self-destructive behavior. Darwin certainly understood this. A critical pillar of his theory of natural selection depends on the resistance to an agent's survival and reproductive aggression by its competitors in the struggle for existence. On the other hand, if there are no competitors, unrestrained selfishness will prevail.

So let us now return to economics, where the issue under the microscope will be the question of wealth and income inequality, a capitalist anomaly that can be as injurious as an invasive species.

Income and Wealth Inequality

The idea of income and wealth inequality has been receiving a considerable amount of attention in both the academic and popular press. But is *inequality* the right term? I think not. This word has been egregiously misappropriated and inaccurately used by people who really want to describe the condition of the economy as one not of *inequality* but rather one of *unfairness*. To my knowledge, none of the critics of capitalism are advocating equality of incomes that would lead to the proven failures of socialism. No, they are really critical of the distribution of wealth and income among various classes, or quintiles, of the population, generally accepting the need for gradation but asking the question, Is it fair?

It is my opinion that the question of income and wealth inequality (i.e., fairness) is the single most important socioeconomic matter confronting contemporary America. I say that because inequality has become so extreme and its extrapolation so seemingly inexorable that

CHARLES L. LADNER

absent intervention, it threatens the very existence of our republic as we know it. The danger comes in several forms:

1. **Corruption:** The risk that the wealthy, to serve their own interests, will readily influence legislatures or government officials by monetary or other comparable means. Some people call this bribery. Employing legal stratagems, it is occurring now, there are no barriers to its proliferation and continued escalation. For example, think of campaign contributions; promises to both elected officials and government employees of high-paying jobs upon retirement; payments for speeches, books, or event appearances; and contributions to fabricated charities providing employment to favored consultants, relatives, and friends of the government official or politician. The list is endless.

2. **Low growth:** There is a growing body of evidence that income and wealth inequality are closely correlated to declining economic growth.

3. **Civic disorder:** The risk of social strife. This, too, is simmering just below the surface, and there are no barriers to its eruption.

When we read that in 2016 only 10% of American households owned 77% of all the nation's privately owned wealth while the remaining 90% owned but 23% of the nation's wealth, we sense an unfair split.[99] And when we see that the top 1% of the population had average household income of about $1.8 million while the other 99% had an annual average income equal to about 5% of what the top 1%, earned, we again sense that something is wrong. Finally, when we read that from 1979 to 2016 the income of the top 1% grew by 226% while the income of the remaining 99% of the population grew by 61%, we are convinced that something is seriously amiss.[100] See table 12 below for additional detail:

---

99   See table 8.

100 Chad Stone, Danilo Trisi, Arloc Sherman, and Jennifer Beltrain, *A Guide to Statistics on Historical Trends in Income Inequality* (Washington, DC: Center on Budget and Policy Priorities, 2020).

Table 12. US Household Income and Gini Coefficients 1979–2016

($000s) 2016 Dollars	Bottom Quintile	2nd Quintile	3rd Quintile	4th Quintile	Top Quintile	Top 1%	Gini
1979							
Market Income	10.0	31.0	53.0	74.0	143.0	558.0	**0.397**
Income after Tax and Transfer	19.0	33.0	47.0	61.0	107.0	366.0	**0.306**
% Difference	**90%**	**6%**	**-11%**	**-18%**	**-25%**	**-34%**	
2016							
Market Income	16.0	33.0	59.0	97.0	280.0	1,779.0	**0.488**
Income after Tax and Transfer	35.0	48.0	66.0	92.0	215.0	1,194.0	**0.354**
% Difference	**119%**	**45%**	**12%**	**-5%**	**-23%**	**-33%**	
Change 1979	16	15	19	31	108	828	
% Change 1979	**84%**	**45%**	**40%**	**51%**	**101%**	**226%**	
CAGR 1979–2016[101]	**1.66%**	**1.02%**	**.92%**	**1.12%**	**1.9%**	**3.25%**	

Source of data: Congressional Budget Office, "The Distribution of Household Income, 2016" (March 2018), www.cbo,gov/ publication/53597.

To better understand table 12, the reader should be aware that all income and wealth data in this table, as well as in all subsequent tables in this book, are expressed in 2016 constant dollars to eliminate the effect of inflation. Also, the following definitions should be helpful:

---

101 CAGR is the compound annual growth rate. Here shown for income after taxes and transfers (1979–2016) as a point of reference, the CAGR of the United States per capita real GDP over the same period was 1.63%.

- *Market income.* This is labor income, business income, capital income (including capital gains), pensions and retirement income, and other nongovernmental sources of income.
- *Income after transfers and taxes.* This the household income after (1) subtracting all individual income taxes, payroll taxes, corporate income taxes, and excise taxes and (2) adding in all cash payments such as Social Security, Medicare, unemployment insurance, and workers compensation, as well as all means-tested cash payments and in-kind transfers provided through federal, state, and local government assistance programs, including such items as Medicaid, Medicare, Children's Health Insurance Program, Food Stamp Program, Supplemental Social Income (SSI), and other smaller programs.
- *Households.* The federal government defined a household in 2016 as comprising 2.6 persons. In 2016, there were 126 million households. Each quintile comprises approximately twenty-five million households or sixty-five million individuals, and 1.0% is 1.26 million households or 3.3 million individuals.
- *CAGR.* This refers to the compound annual growth rate.

Now as to the contents of the table, by 1979, it is clear that the Great Society welfare programs of the 1960s had accomplished their purpose, for the twenty-five million people then comprising the lowest quintile of the population saw their income after tax and transfers nearly double by reason of welfare payments. Their income rose from $10,000 per household to $19,000. To put that into perspective, in 1979, the United States government poverty threshold was approximately $5,000 per household. This may be compared to the bottom quintile's 1979 income after taxes and transfers of $19,000. Therefore, I think it can be reasonably said that whatever responsibility society felt in the past toward the welfare of the bottom quintile appears to be fully satisfied by 1979 (although the distribution of income and benefits within the quintile may have been problematic).

This conclusion is well supported by the Gini coefficients. In 1979, the market income Gini was .397. This is high and indicative of an unfair or inequitable distribution of income. But after applying taxes and benefits that added considerable income to the lowest groups at the expense of the middle and highest income groups, the Gini moved down to .306, which is indicative of an equitable and fair distribution of income.

However, when we move forward to 2016, the picture changes. As in 1979, the bottom quintile did very well. In fact, it did better. Its improvement in income for that year, from social and welfare transfers, was 119%. This group, the bottom quintile, saw its income more than double, mainly at the expense of everyone else. The next three quintiles, which comprise the middle class, saw the net of their taxes and transfers increase their income by only 17%.

In the 1980s and in the following decades, both personal and corporate tax policies were radically changed to favor the wealthy and upper classes. These changes were mainly subsidized by the middle class. Consider this: Over the course of the thirty-seven years between 1979 and 2016, the compound annual growth rate (CAGR) of the United States GDP (in 2016 constant dollars) was approximately 1.6% per year. During that same period, household income after taxes and transfers grew at a compound annual rate of 1.45% per year. But the distribution was uneven. The bottom quintile, as might be expected, did well; its CAGR was 1.66%. Over the same thirty-seven years, the top quintile experienced a 1.9% CAGR, while the top 1% enjoyed a 3.24% CAGR. Meanwhile, the middle quintiles—the middle class—did not keep up with the growth of the economy. Their CAGR was but 1.02%.

Moreover, when we evaluate the fairness, or inequality, of the 2016 economy against the 1979 economy, we find an unmistakable deterioration. In 1979, the Gini for income after taxes and transfers was .306. By 2016, it had risen to .354. As a rough gauge of what it would take to produce the same .306 Gini of 1979 in 2016, the income after taxes and transfers of the top quintile would have to be reduced from $215,000 to $182,000 and the top 1.0% would have to come down from $1.2 million to $624,000. Coincidentally, these reductions would also have resulted in the CAGR of these top incomes equaling the 1.6% CAGR of the economy as a whole.

So if we are concerned about the risks to the economy as noted earlier and, therefore, if fairness or better income equality is the goal, then the answer seems obvious. Just increase income taxes on the rich and redistribute the proceeds to the middle class. Problem solved!

Oh, if the matter were so simple.

Well, it's not. Let us return to the biological imperatives that initiated our study and see what they mean for income gradations, economic growth, and prosperity.

The Justification for Gradations in Income

As the reader now knows, this book is nothing more than a simple inquiry regarding the application of the theory of natural selection to economics. It is grounded on the science of evolutionary biology, and as such, it treats human economic behavior not merely as a social analog of natural selection but rather as the direct biological product of natural selection. There is a difference. All the preceding discussions in this book suggest that the instincts of selfishness that generate the results of natural selection are deterministic and irrevocably dictate the results of economic systems. Thus, we have seen that socialism is biologically predetermined to fail, while capitalism, at least to a point, is biologically predetermined to succeed. The reservations expressed about capitalism relate to the societal reluctance to control the self-destructive tendencies of unrestrained capitalist selfishness, which I identify as (1) excessive inequality of income and wealth, (2) environmental despoliation, and (3) monopolization.

The question of monopolies was adequately settled in the late nineteenth century. All that remains is the political will to enforce the existing laws. The environmental matters are well publicized but not well in hand, although the political and public momentum appears to be on the right track. On the other hand, notwithstanding the extensive conversation in the academic community, the matter of income and wealth inequality are presently nowhere to be found in the nation's political agenda.

In a recent book on the topic of allometric scaling as applied to the development of cities, physicist Geoffrey West insightfully proposed a slightly different formulation of the instinctive selfishness that has been the principal topic of this book. He speaks of

> the insatiable drive of individuals, small businesses, and giant companies to always want more. Or, to put it in crass terms, the socioeconomic machinery that we all participate in is primarily fueled by greed, in both its negative and positive connotations as in the sense of the "desire for more." Given the enormous disparities in income distribution in all cities across the globe, and the apparent drive of most of us to want more despite having plenty, it's not hard to believe that greed in its various forms is an important contributor to the socioeconomic dynamics of cities.[102]

From the perspective of this study, Geoffrey West's insight is that greed (or selfishness) compels all participants in the economic arena to always want more despite having plenty.

It is precisely this formulation that explains why income gradation is necessary. Capitalism cannot function without aspirational motivation. To want more despite having plenty sounds morally repugnant (and in many cases, it is). Yet this compulsion, which is embedded in the biological blueprint of every living thing, is the critical instrumentality that enables society to attain material benefits unapproachable in any economic system other than capitalism.

Thus, the practical dilemma for all of us, no matter how offended we may be by excessive greed, is that we know, from the experience of history, that capitalism—with its indispensable income inequality—can provide the highest standards of living for the greatest number of people (subject only to a just distribution). So it seems that for the greater good,

---

102 Geoffrey West, *Scale: The Universal Laws of Life, Growth, and Death in Organisms, Cities, and Companies* (New York: Penguin Random House LLC, 2017), 286–7.

we must be prepared to accept the morally compromising fact of income inequality and work within that scheme to assure fairness.

And therein lies the challenge—that is, finding the most equitable distribution of income possible without eroding the motivational properties of income gradation.

An Analysis of the Inequality Problem in the United States

Theory and broad concepts like those so favored by Marxists are useless for this exercise. History, on the other hand, is the key. We know, for example, that on a comparative scale, the United States has an unfair income Gini of .414, while the Nordic countries and most Northern European countries are much more equitable, running between .270 to .300 (see table 2). We also know that overall income in these countries is roughly equal to the United States as attested by comparing the United States GDP per capita of $63,000 with the Nordic and Northern European countries, where it runs between $49,000 and $67,000. Economists call the European model social democratic capitalism. It works well for its constituents, so something like it should work equally well for the United States.

Historical experience informs us that by emulating the European social democratic economies, the United States could reduce its Gini to approximately .300 without impairing growth or general prosperity. This would require a redistribution of income from the top quintile to those below it. However, before unconditionally embracing this idea, we should be aware that none of the social democratic economies have exhibited the extraordinary level of innovation that has occurred within the American tech industry. And we should ask ourselves how much of this entrepreneurial innovation is the result of the stimulation provided by an expectation of extraordinary financial rewards. There can be no doubt that the critical venture capital industry is so stimulated, and the same may be said about the entrepreneurs and company founders, but it may not be so certain regarding the scientists and researchers.

Nevertheless, it seems obvious that the lure and potential realization of high incomes act as a powerful stimulus to commercial innovation; and absent such incentives, one can legitimately question whether widespread technological advances we now enjoy ever would have occurred. Remember, there's no Silicon Valley in Europe!

Moreover, none of these social democratic countries are encumbered with the obligation to support international stability to the same level of engagement as the United States. For these reasons, the idea of a straightforward redistribution of income, which could damage the US economy's incentive structure, presents too much risk to seriously consider. Rather, I would suggest that the objective of creating a more fair and equitable society, similar to the European model (without its regressive value-added tax), would be better achieved not so much by radically penalizing the top income brackets but rather by finding most of the needed funding through taxation of inherited wealth, which, unlike income gradation, serves no useful socioeconomic purpose.

In the next few pages, I will lay out in broad strokes the general principles and possible actions that could achieve the objective of improved income equality, coupled with substantial social benefits, in a way that assures success. To assert assurance of success is a bold statement. But it is one that is supported by the findings of everything that precedes it in this study, for it is uniquely predicated on a schematic that is fully congruent with genetically derived motivation of human selfishness.

This analysis, along with the tables that illustrate it, is constructed using data published by the Congressional Budget Office (CBO). The CBO data is not quite as complete as that provided by Piketty, Saez, and Zucman used in chapter 10, but it offers two distinct advantages: first, it provides a detailed breakdown of income groups by quintile and second, it uses US government data from the Internal Revenue Service, the Census Bureau, and the Federal Reserve, which is more likely to be the basis for policy formulation. The tables and the commentary should be read sequentially, because, in a derivative logic, they present the kernel of an argument to reform US tax policy for the two-fold purpose of achieving economic fairness by reducing inequality and rescuing the capitalist system from its own self-destructive tendencies.

The first table in this sequence (table 13) tells us what happened to the income of each of the quintiles and the top 1% from 1979 through 2016.

Table 13. Income after Tax and Transfer 1979–2016 (2016 constant dollars)

Year	Bottom Quintile	2nd Quintile	3rd Quintile	4th Quintile	Top Quintile	Top 1%	Gini
1979 Income after Tax and Transfer	$19,000	$33,000	$47,000	$61,000	$107,000	$366,000	0.306
2016 Income after Tax and Transfer	$35,000	$48,000	$66,000	$92,000	$215,000	$1,194,000	0.354
Change from 1979	$16,000	$15,000	$19,000	$31,000	$108,000	$828,000	
Change from 1979	84%	45%	40%	51%	101%	226%	
CAGR	1.66%	1.02%	0.92%	1.12%	1.90%	3.25%	

Source: CBO, *The Distribution of Household Income, 2016*, and author's calculations.

Over the span of thirty-seven years from 1979 to 2016, the US GDP per capita grew at a compound annual growth rate (CAGR) of approximately 1.6%, which produced a compound annual growth of Income after Tax and Transfer of 1.45%. Table 13 applies the 1.45% CAGR to each of the income quintiles to determine whether the growth of GDP and Income after Tax and Transfers was fairly distributed to all classes. As may be seen, the income benefits were *not* fairly distributed. The income after taxes and transfers of the bottom quintile improved. It did so mainly by increases in transfers, primarily means-tested welfare benefits, and, thus, correctly reflected the growth in the economy. On the other hand, the middle three quintiles, which comprise the middle class, fell behind, while the top quintile and especially the top 1%, influenced by federal tax policies designed to improve top quintile disposable income opportunities, increased at a much greater rate than justified by the growth in the economy. The disproportionate concentration of income benefits in top quintile incomes pushed up the Gini from .306 to .354, which reveals a significant emergence of economic injustice. What is interesting, however, is that this picture exposes something that has not been widely recognized in public conversation, and that is the unmistakable fact that the growth in the income of the top 1% was made possible by redistribution from the middle class. Said candidly, the prosperity and affluence of the upper class has been subsidized by the stagnation of the middle class. So look once again at the bottom row of figures and see whose situation improved and whose did not.

The next table (table 14) illustrates income tax and social benefit changes that could rectify the disservice done to the middle class. It describes what would have been the outcome had tax policies been designed to fairly distribute all incomes in proportion to economic growth. When viewing this data, it is important to recall that the tax policies initiated in the mid-1980s favoring the higher income groups were originally designed with the expectation that they would stimulate higher economic growth and that this would benefit all income classes because the expected economic gains would trickle down to everyone's advantage.

Well, the score is now in; and as it turned out, the hoped-for economic growth never materialized and trickle-down proved to be a myth.

Table 14. Income after Tax and Transfer 1979–2016 at the GDP/Capita Thirty-Seven-Year Compound Annual Growth Rate of 1.45%

Year	Bottom Quintile	2nd Quintile	3rd Quintile	4th Quintile	Top Quintile	Top 1%	Gini
1979 Income after Tax and Transfer	$19,000	$33,000	$47,000	$61,000	$107,000	$366,000	0.306
2016 Income after Tax and Transfer	$35,000	$48,000	$66,000	$92,000	$215,000	$1,194,000	0.354
Hypothetical 2016 Income after Tax and Transfer at 1.45% CAGR	$32,000	$56,000	$80,000	$104,000	$182,000	$624,000	0.306
Change from 2016 Actual	($3,000)	$8,000	$14,000	$12,000	($33,000)	($570,000)	
% Change	(7.5)%	17.1%	21.3%	12.9%	(15.3)%	(47.8)%	

Source: CBO, *The Distribution of Household Income, 2016*, and author's calculations.

In the above table (table 14), each quintile represents 25.2 million households. If we multiply the change from 2016 for the second quintile ($8,000) by the number of households in that quintile, we will find that the difference is $202 billion. And if we do the same calculation for all three of the quintiles, which constitute the middle class, we will find that the total is $857 billion. Said differently, if one accepts the notion that all income classes ought to share proportionately in the overall national prosperity, then there is a big problem. There is a problem because in a single year, 2016 for example, the bottom quintile and the top quintile saw their incomes enhanced at the expense of the middle class, who effectively subsidized the other two classes by an involuntary reduction in their potential income. In 2016, it was by $857 billion, or an average of $11,300 per household. Again, I would like to remind the reader that before attributing questionable motives, we should recall that an outcome quite so distorted was not the intent of the mid-1980s and subsequent tax changes. But nevertheless, what were undoubtedly the good intentions of trickle-down sharing of benefits (fueled by supply-side theories) were badly misguided. Trickle-down never materialized.

Figure 3. Increase in Annual Income after Tax and Transfers for 2016 over 1979 by Quintile and the Top 1%

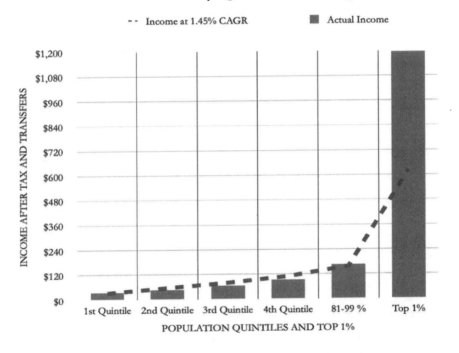

The chart at figure 3, drawn from tables 13 and 14, illustrates in inflation-adjusted dollars the extent of the imbalance. For example, look at the third quintile. Here we see that the income after tax and transfer for these people went up by $19,000 $66,000, but if it had kept up with the 1.45% compound growth in the total income, it would have gone up by $33,000 per year to $80,000. Now compare that to the 1.0%, whose annual income went up to $1.2 million, when if it grew in tandem with the economy, it would have risen to $624,000. The difference is $570,000 per year. But above all, the key takeaway from this chart (figure 3) is the presence of extreme income inequality even within the top quintile. The visualization leads nicely into the data on table 15 where it may be seen that the average income after tax and transfers of people in the 81–99 percentile is approximately $167,000, while that of the top 1.0% is $1.2 million—seven times greater.

Injustice is deeply embedded all throughout the income quintiles, reaching its apogee at the top 1%. But it can be repaired. It can be repaired by a changes in taxation of the top 1% to fund redistribution to the middle class, either indirectly by such things as Medicare-for-all or subsidization of college tuitions or directly by tax credits through expansion and revision of the earned income tax credit (EITC). I would favor the latter because it would result in a more fair and uniform distribution of benefits.

However, notwithstanding the disproportionate consequence of past tax policy favoring the upper class, one can legitimately question whether such remedies as suggested above are in the best interests of the economy as a whole. Traditionally, the argument for the upper class receiving an unequal share of income is that it is the natural outcome of higher economic growth. Well, if that is correct, the data should prove it. So let's take a look at the numbers.

In 1979, the distribution of income was moderately balanced with a Gini of .306. Yet there was still significant gradation, as the top 1% income of $366,000 (after taxes and transfers) was six times that of the fourth percentile income of $61,000. As for economic performance, the compound annual growth rate (CAGR) of GDP per capita over the previous thirty-three years from the end of World War II through 1979 was 2.23%; and even for the decade of the 1970s, which was blemished by unusually high and disruptive inflation, the CAGR was 2.23%. All that time, the Gini remained stable at around .300.

Now move forward to 2016. After thirty seven years of supply-side economics and the promise of trickle-down growth, we find the distribution of incomes has negatively changed. The Gini has moved up to .354, and the ratio of top 1.0% income is now thirteen times more than that of the fourth quintile. Moreover, despite expectations to the contrary, the economic performance was disappointing. For the thirty-seven years from 1979 through 2016, a period during which income tax policies were liberalized in favor of the rich, the CAGR was 1.64%—a considerable underperformance when compared to the 2.23% of the preceding period.

All this proves nothing other than to suggest that in a mature economy, there comes a point where increasing income inequality cannot be correlated with higher rates of economic growth; and in fact, it may actually reverse or suppress it (as it seems to have done in the 1979–2016 period).[103]

That said, it would appear that the balanced income distribution of the United States in the immediate postwar years (as well as that of most Western European countries in the present time) should be a logical standard to mark a level of economic justice that appears to be absent in the early twenty-first century in the United States. In addition, using the 1979 income distribution as the standard to create redistributive tax policies and thus moving toward a more equitable and more just economy will not only mitigate the social discontent lying beneath the surface, which presents a not inconsequential risk to civic order but of equal importance, but also may possibly result in a higher rate of growth that supply-side economics did not deliver.

Such a standard can be met only by aggressive redistribution, and aggressive redistribution can be implemented only through aggressive tax policy. However, as will be described in the following tables, if it is attempted solely through the income tax, the degree of tax changes required over a relatively short period of time may be a bridge too far. It took over thirty years for the United States to put itself in this untenable condition, but to bite off the entire problem at one time could

---

103 See Thomas Piketty, *Capital and Ideology*, trans. Arthur Goldhammer (Cambridge MA: Harvard University press, 2020), 543–546. Piketty's findings regarding the periods 1870–1910, 1910–1950, 1950–1990, and 1990–2020 display a consistent negative correlation between income inequality and growth of national income in both Europe and the United States for all periods. These recent findings are an important confirmation of my findings that too much inequality produces low growth.

CHARLES L. LADNER

be politically impossible and would certainly be disruptive, yet there appears to be little tolerance to take thirty years to clean it up.

In the next few pages, I will outline tax increases applied not just to income, as has been our practice in the United States, but also to wealth, which is something that has never been done in this country. Moreover, to be consistent with the objective of redistribution, the wealth tax would be imposed principally on the large concentrations of wealth (i.e., the top 1%) and also to the enormous pools of financial assets under management, including the heretofore untouchable large nonprofit funds. I will address these ideas through a series of tables that illustrate the proposition by walking through the logic step-by-step. Since it is the wealthy who will carry this additional tax burden, these tables isolate the changes to the top quintile and thus show how tax changes may occur by demonstrating their affordability for each category within the top quintile. Table 15 sets forth household income as it actually occurred within the top quintile. Table 16 depicts the impact of an effective tax rate required if income taxes are the sole means to address the problem of inequality, and it illustrates why such an approach is unrealistic because it results in an effective rate of about 63%, which when combined with state taxes could result in an overall effective rate in the neighborhood of 70%.[104] Table 17 presents a compromise income tax solution that, though realistically possible, still yields insufficient funds to correct the problem and thus not only demonstrates the futility of addressing the matter solely through income taxes but also points to the necessity of a tax on wealth.

---

104 To understand the impossibility of this rate of taxation, we should remember that in 2016, the highest statutory marginal rate was 39.6% but the actual taxes collected, or what is called the effective rate, was 26.9%. Even in 1979, when the top marginal rate was 70.0%, the effective rate was about 22.0%. It would be naive in the extreme to expect that any elected legislated body would move the effective rate from 26.9% to, say, 63.0% as shown in table 16.

Table 15. Deconstruction of the Top Quintile Income for 2016

Table 15	Top Quintile	81–90 Percentile	91–95 Percentile	96–99 Percentile	Top 1%
Market Income	$280,300	$148,100	$208,000	$349,300	$1,779,200
Social Insurance Benefits	$10,900	$11,500	$10,400	$10,200	$9,600
Income before Taxes and Transfers	$291,200	$159,600	$218,300	$359,500	$1,788,800
Means-Tested Transfers	$1,000	$1,100	$900	$800	$1,000
Federal Taxes	$77,300	$33,800	$51,600	$96,300	$595,900
Income after Taxes and Transfers	$214,900	$126,800	$167,700	$264,100	$1,193,900
Federal Tax %	26.5%	21.2%	23.6%	26.8%	33.3%

Source: CBO, *The Distribution of Household Income, 2016*, and author's calculations.

Before going any further, it may be helpful to understand just what kind of professions fall within these percentiles. We tend to think of the top quintile as comprising the uber-rich. Well, that's just not so. Examples of people in the 81–90 percentile are such professions as midlevel corporate executives, judges, pharmacists, personal financial advisers, attorneys, architects, engineering managers, podiatrists, and information technology managers. Those in the 91–95 percentile are dentists, pediatricians, internists, midlevel executives, school superintendents, and college professors. In the 96–99 percentile are found such professions as surgeons, orthopedic specialists, gastroenterologists, small college presidents, senior corporate executives, and hospital administrators. Finally, in the top 1%, where the household income threshold is approximately $400–$500,000 per year, typical examples may be investment bankers, CEOs, bond traders, university presidents, senior partners in large law firms, business owners, real estate developers, sports and entertainment figures, television newscasters and commentators, former United States presidents, and of course, the idle rich: the inheritors of great fortunes and children of rich parents. Also within the top 1% are 630 billionaires, whose collective wealth is $3.4 trillion and whose average wealth per household is about $5.4 billion.

The whole purpose of this listing of the Who's Who of the top quintile is to point out that all but the top 1% are ordinary people whom we all encounter in everyday life. Like all of us, they go to work and they have home mortgages and worry about making ends meet. Most live in middle-class neighborhoods and live a middle-class lifestyle. They are assuredly not the plutocrats of popular imagination.

However, when it comes to the top 1%, the 1,260,000 most affluent households, we are in an entirely different universe. But even in this group, there exists extreme stratification by income and wealth. The averages tend to hide the reality. Meaningful and substantial income and wealth differentiation does not occur until one reaches the top 0.1%, the 126,000 wealthiest households. For example, whereas the average annual income of the top 1.0% in total is about $1.8 million, when we break it down, the average income of the top 0.1% runs about $12 million, while the average annual income of the remaining .089% is approximately $645,000. Also, while the wealth threshold of the top 1.0% is about $4 million, the wealth threshold of the top 0.1% is estimated to be about $20 million. Moreover, while the average wealth of the top .01% is estimated at $73 million, the average wealth of the remaining .089% is estimated to be about $7 million. None of these people are starving; however, it is from this top group, the top 0.1%, those who have most generously benefitted by the tax policies of the last thirty-seven years favoring the wealthy, that the middle class can justly look for redress, and it can do so without seriously damaging the motivational values of income and wealth gradations. Tables 18 and 19 will illustrate how this may be possible.

A Pragmatic Solution[105]

At the outset, I would like to stipulate that these tables and the proposed corrective measures to the problem of income inequality in the United States are presented as but one possibility out of many. And in that light, the reader is cautioned to view this exercise as a sort of laboratory test to validate the feasibility of the concept. The idea works. That is to say, the math works. But it is hypothetical and does not constitute a fully developed proposition.

First, let us look at table 16. This table is an extension of table 14 that calculates the income distribution that would result if the income in all quintiles increased from 1979 to 2016 at the same rate: a CAGR of 1.45%. Table 16 applies this same process, except this time within the top quintile, to determine the results for the several segment comprising the top quintile, with the bulk of the tax increase allocated to the top 1% who have the group that gained the most from the tax policies of the 1979–2016 period. In both cases, tables 14 and 16, the process mechanically forces all changes into the federal tax line, because that is where any applied changes would most likely occur.

---

105 Many of the ideas in this chapter, including even the title of this section, are drawn from the following paper published by the Hamilton Project: Natasha Sarin, Lawrence A. Summers, and Joel Kupferberg, *Tax Reform for Progressivity: A Pragmatic Approach* (Washington, DC: The Hamilton Project, January 28, 2020), accessed July 9, 2020, www.Hamiltonproject.org/assets/files/SarinSommers_LO_FINAL.pdf.

CHARLES L. LADNER

Table 16. Pro Forma Deconstruction of the Top Quintile Income for 2016 with Income Tax Changes to Produce a .306 Gini for All Quintiles and a Uniform 1.45% CAGR for All Quintiles from 1979

Table 16	Top Quintile	81–90 Percentile	91–95 Percentile	96–99 Percentile	Top 1%
Market Income	$280,300	$148,100	$208,000	$349,300	$1,779,200
Social Insurance Benefits	$10,900	$11,500	$10,400	$10,200	$9,600
Income before Taxes and Transfers	$291,200	$159,600	$218,300	$359,500	$1,788,800
Means-Tested Transfers	$1,000	$1,100	$900	$800	$1,000
Federal Taxes	$110,200	$24,700	$61,200	$127,300	$1,164,800
Income after Taxes and Transfers	$182,000	$136,000	$158,000	$233,000	$624,000
Federal Tax %	37.8%	15.5%	27.8%	35.4%	65.1%

Comparing this table (table 16) with table 15, we can see that within the top quintile, the 96–99 percentile would experience a reduction in income after tax and transfer of $31,000 from $264,000 to $233,000—a reduction of 11.7%. The effective federal tax rate would rise from 26.8% to 34.6%. At the same time, the top 1.0% would experience a vastly greater change. Here there would be a reduction in income after tax and transfer of $570,000 from $1,194,000 to $624,000—a reduction of 47.7%. The effective tax rate would rise from 33.3% to 65.1%, and would generate approximately $830 billion in additional federal revenues. 16

I believe there is little possibility that changes of this magnitude would be legislated. Even in 1960, when the maximum marginal rate reached 91%, the effective rate (including state taxes) never exceeded 47%. Thus, an effective rate of 65.1% is so absurdly out of line as to be unthinkable.[106] This implies that there is a practical limit to how much can be done to correct the imbalance in inequality solely through taxes on income.

A Generalized Proposal for Increased Income Taxes to the 1%

Table 17, which follows, displays a compromise pragmatic approach that seems more realistic than the ideas expressed in table 16. This table is constructed by moving the increased effective tax rate on the top 1% to 45%. It also increases the effective tax rate for the 96–99 percentile to 34.9% and corrects the distortion in the 81–90 percentile that occurred in table 16's mechanical rendition. The total increase in pro forma federal taxes is $387 billion. This is a big help, but keep in mind that fully correcting the inequity imposed on the middle classes requires a total of $860 billion in redistribution from the top quintile, so while the $387 billion is a meaningful first step, it does not get the job done.

---

106 Sarin (2020), 319.

Table 17. Pro Forma Deconstruction of the Top Quintile Income for 2016 with Pragmatic Changes in Income Taxes

Table 17	Top Quintile	81–90 Percentile	91–95 Percentile	96–99 Percentile	Top 1%
Market Income	$280,300	$148,100	$208,000	$349,300	$1,779,200
Social Insurance Benefits	$10,900	$11,500	$10,400	$10,200	$9,600
Income before Taxes and Transfers	$291,200	$159,600	$218,300	$359,500	$1,788,000
Means-Tested Transfers	$1,000	$1,100	$900	$800	$1,000
Federal Taxes	$92,685	$29,600	$51,900	$124,400	$800,600
Income after Taxes and Transfers	$199,515	$131,100	$167,300	$235,900	$988,400
Federal Tax %	31.8%	18.5%	23.8%	34.6%	44.8%

Are these changes realistic? Can they be achieved? I believe they are. The Sarin, Summers, and Kupferberg paper referenced in note 110 lays out a number of practical, pragmatic, and thus, legislatively possible improvements to federal tax law and administration. Such an approach to tax reform by highly credible scholars readily supports the possibility of achieving an overall increase in federal revenues of the $387 billion as shown in table 17 (and probably a lot more). Here is a brief summary of some of their suggestions, along with my pro forma estimate of annual realization. The Sarin, Summers, and Kupferberg paper follows the conventional method of valuing federal budget proposals by showing the ten-year effect of each proposal. This has the benefit of smoothing out the ramp-up period as well as the inflationary and economic growth assumptions. However, I prefer a pro forma approach that takes an average amount for a single year and applies to a pro forma base, which is the year 2016 in tables 15–19.

Pro Forma Revenue Potential of Proposed Programs as Set Forth by Sarin, Summers, and Kupferberg (2020)[107]

Program	2016 Pro Forma ($ billions)
• Enforcement, information reporting, and technology	117
• Corporate taxes	77
• Capital gains	82
• Closing individual loopholes and shelters	<u>130</u>
Total	**406**

None of these recommendations are especially radical. For example, the first recommendation comes down to simply operating the Internal Revenue Service in a way that comports with its statutory mission. This requires nothing more than adequate funding and competent management. This alone can provide more than $100 billion per year in additional tax revenues. It's what's often called a low-hanging fruit.[108]

Reforming corporate taxation may be more difficult, but some changes are obvious: eliminating the subchapter S option, eliminating like-kind exchanges, and requiring a minimum tax on book earnings. Other changes, for competitive reasons, may be more problematic, as, for example, raising the corporate tax rate to a level that puts US corporations at a disadvantage against foreign competitors.

On the other hand, at the individual level, there truly is a low-hanging fruit—for instance, taxing carried interests at ordinary income tax levels or taxing dividends above a given level, say, $1 million, at ordinary income levels and doing the same for capital gains. Then there is the 20% pass-through deduction, a product of the 2017 Tax Cuts and Jobs Act (TCJA). This was not in place in 2016 (our pro forma year), but

---

107 Sarin (2020), 318.
108 Sarin (2020), 322–332.

eliminating this provision (that serves no discernible economic purpose other than to benefit the wealthy) could correct an estimated $43 billion tax loss to the Treasury.[109]

Finally, we come to the estate tax.[110] To get a sense of the order of magnitude, it is currently projected that in 2020, the total amount of inheritances will be $765 billion. Moreover, notwithstanding the common belief that aggregate wealth is mainly the output of self-made individuals, it is estimated that about 40% of all such wealth was derived from inheritances.[111] So the estate tax is very important. Yet while the statutory rate at 40% seems high, it is applicable to estates only in excess of $23.2 million per couple. And even then, the remaining taxable estate after exemptions is typically sheltered from taxation by such strategies as the application of nonliquidity discounts in combination with family offices, grantor, and generation-skipping trusts. The net effect is to produce an effective tax rate of approximately 2% on all estates and gifts.[112]

There is clearly something wrong with this, not least of which is extraordinary distributive injustice. But it can be corrected. New York University School of Law professor Lily Batchelder has been developing a new and most promising theory of estate taxation. She proposes eliminating the current structure of estate taxes in which it is the decedent's estate that is taxed and substituting an income tax paid by the heir(s) on the inheritance. The idea is brilliant in its simplicity. When the heir or legatee receives an inheritance, he/she is receiving income, so isn't it fair and just that the heir or legatee includes this income (the received inheritance) in that year's 1040 tax return and pay the appropriate income tax? After all, everyone else, including even a lottery winner, pays income taxes on income received, so why should this income be

---

109 Sarin (2020), 334–340.

110 The principal reference in this section is this: Lily Batchelder, "Leveling the Playing Field between Inherited Income and Income from Work through an Inheritance Tax," in *Tackling the Tax Code: Efficient and Equitable Ways to Raise Revenue*, ed. Jay Shambaugh and Ryan Nunn (Washington, DC: The Hamilton Project, 2020).

111 Batchelder (2020), 46.

112 Batchelder (2020), 46, 61–64.

an exception? Also, and this is critical, the definition of heir or legatee should encompass not just individuals but also all entities receiving a bequest, including such entities as trusts and charitable institutions.

Among other things, Batchelder's proposal eliminates the need for a step-up in basis because the market value is the basis on which the income tax would be paid. Batchelder has worked out the issues regarding the payment of taxes when there is insufficient liquidity in the inheritance, and she has dealt with the matter of trust, family limited partnerships, and discounts normally applied to the valuation of illiquid assets. To soften the blow and in consideration of smaller estates, she proposes the heir receive a lifetime exemption of up to $2.5 million before applying the income tax. I do not see the need for this. Like "a rose is a rose," income is income, so just like anyone who is paid wages, tax it all. However, even with the $2.5 million exemption, her proposal could generate, on a pro forma calculation, upward of $34 billion per year over and above today's revenue yield.

These studies, which I reference in very brief summary—that is to say, the work of Sarin, Summers, and Kupferberg, along with that of Lily Batchelder—provide, in my view, sufficient evidence from highly credible sources that the proposed increase in income taxation of $257 billion to the top 1% is not out of the realm of possibility. But it is inadequate to the task, so that leaves the taxation of wealth as the only alternative to achieving distributive justice and rectifying the damage done to the middle class.

Taxation of Wealth

Unlike the taxation of income, the taxation of wealth has no precedent in the United States; and even if limited only to the top 1%, it would meet with great resistance. The introduction of such an idea would, of course, be met with the emotional slippery-slope arguments that if a wealth tax were to be imposed on the uber-rich, "it would be only a matter of time before everyone's wealth is attacked, retirement funds would be demolished, savings and personal assets would be expropriated, freedom bound up in property rights would disappear, and we all would become slaves to a totalitarian socialist state.: But once beyond all that balderdash, there are some quite legitimate and well-founded objections to a wealth tax. Many are grounded on the recent European experience.

Most of the difficulties that taxing authorities have encountered with wealth taxes center on problems of valuation, capital mobility, and underreporting. Valuation issues arise when attempting to tax illiquid assets such as equity in privately owned firms, objects of art, yachts, and collectables. Capital mobility refers to the ease with which the wealthy taxpayer can move assets to offshore tax havens or other low-tax jurisdictions. Underreporting is a form of tax evasion that entails obfuscation of records, the use of multiple entities to hold assets, and outright fraud.

To avoid or at least minimize these problems, the following proposal taxes only two classes of assets: marketable securities (including private equity) and residential real estate, including the capitalized value of rented residential properties. The problems encountered by European authorities can be largely avoided by narrowing the taxable assets to those that are immobile and for which there are already excellent recordkeeping practices in place.

To get an understanding of the magnitude of taxable financial assets eligible for taxation, I referenced the Federal Reserve "Balance Sheet of Households and Nonprofit Organizations" for 2016 (the pro forma year) to identify total financial assets of households and nonprofits at $77.2 trillion. From this amount, I subtracted the asset categories that are most likely to be held by the middle class: checkable deposits and currency, time and savings deposits, mutual fund shares, and pension assets.[113] This leaves $35.3 trillion, most of which is held by custodian banks or financial institutions. The records pertinent to these assets should be very accurate and complete, which means that movement of assets can be tracked and enforcement should be not difficult. My proposal is to apply a 1.5% annual tax, which would yield about $590

---

113 Federal Reserve, *Financial Accounts of the United States, B.101,* 2020.

billion in the pro forma year. It should be noted that this proposal would include the assets above a predetermined minimum and also include the assets of nonprofit entities, such as college and school endowments, charitable funds, and large foundations.

As for real estate, I again used Federal Reserve data;[114] and isolating the tax to the top 1%, I would propose a graduated scale with total residential real estate holdings, including vacation, and all other residential property valued over $75 million to be taxed at 6% per annum, property valued between $15 and $75 million at 4%, and for the remaining members of the 1%, a tax of 2%. In total, this works out to be a tax of 4.3% on $3.561 trillion of residential real estate assets and would yield annual receipts of approximately $155 billion.

In summary, the total amount for redistribution before allowing for the inevitable leakage from under-reporting, inefficiency, and fraud, could be as much as $1,132 billion for the pro forma year ($387 billion from increased income tax, $590 billion from the financial asset tax, and $155 billion from the real estate mansion tax).

In this exercise, I have attempted to test the reasonableness of a substantial increase in taxes guided by respect for the biological necessity of selfishness, which in practice means preservation of the income gradations serving the vital aspirational motivation that feeds a successful capitalist economy. This logic leads to a program of cautious increases in the taxation of income while simultaneously introducing a strongly progressive and material taxation of wealth, all of which is proposed as a means of reestablishing an economic system that can deliver distributional justice as existed in the United States in years past.

The time has come to seriously address this issue. The current imbalance in the distribution of wealth is unsustainable. Not only is it incompatible with the very founding principles on which our society has been grounded, principles that accord all citizens equal dignity and mutual respect, but also by continuing to protect and prolong the extremes of wealth that so clearly distort the idea of civic equality, we could, and most assuredly would, experience a reaction producing violent

---

114 Federal Reserve, *Distributional Financial Accounts*, 2020.

social discord. And the political outcome of such discord could, and probably would, so severely damage the capitalist system that the nation's economic prosperity would be endangered. In effect, by its success, our capitalist economy is generating its own undoing. It has done so in the past. And in consequence, the political system will either directly confiscate the totality of sterile wealth or the wealth holders themselves will cooperate in its shrinkage and redistribution. So with that in mind, the redistributive concepts embodied in the foregoing model with its novel ideas of wealth taxation are summarized in the following table.

Table 18. The Net Redistributive Effect on Income Inequality from Increased Income and Wealth Taxes on the Top 1% with All Benefits Allocated to the Middle Class (Quintiles 2–4)

	Bottom Quintile	2nd Quintile	3rd Quintile	4th Quintile	Top Quintile	Gini
2016 Income after Tax and Transfer	$35,000	$48,000	$66,000	$92,000	$215,000	.354
2016 Hypothetical Income after Tax and Transfer with 1.45% CAGR (see table 14)	$32,000	$56,000	$80,000	$104,000	$182,000	.306
2016 Pro Forma Income after Tax and Transfer with the Redistribution allocated to the 2nd through 4th Percentiles	$35,000	$63,000	$81,000	$107,000	$200,000	.318

The model shown above is one in which the distribution of benefits is limited only to the second through fourth quintiles, which constitute the middle class. The distribution is $14,974 per household. However, the political reality is such that leaving out the bottom quintile is not feasible. Therefore, distributing the benefits to all but the top quintile would produce the following results.

Table 19. The Net Redistributive Effect on Income Inequality from Increased Income and Wealth Taxes on the Top 1% with Benefits Allocated to All but the Top Quintile

	Bottom Quintile	2nd Quintile	3rd Quintile	4th Quintile	Top Quintile	Gini
2016 Pro Forma Income after Tax and Transfer with Proposed Benefits Distributed to All but the Top Quintile	$46,000	$59,000	$77,000	$103,000	$200,000	.290

Table 19 is the final table of the series. It shows a broad distribution of benefits, which in order to achieve the level of equality integral to this table would have to be in the form of cash, most efficiently delivered through the EITC program. The distribution is made to all but the Top Quintile. The amount is $11,230 per household. Interestingly, it brings the Gini to a position slightly better than 1979 and thus attains the standard of equality that had been advanced as an objective earlier in the text.[115]

The preceding example is not in sufficient detail to be considered as a proposal. Rather, it is simply an exercise to test the feasibility of

---

115 One additional note: There have been objections to the idea of a wealth tax on constitutional grounds. The matter is not settled, but firm support for it has been voiced by the American Bar Association. See Calvin H. Johnson, "A Wealth Tax Is Constitutional," in *ABA Tax Times* 38 no. 4 (Summer 2019), retrieved September 5, 2020, www.americanbar.org/groups/taxation/publications/abataxtimes_home/19aug/.

a possible program to restore economic justice. And in line with this objective, I would like to reinforce the idea that the cure to inequality should be in the form of an annual distribution in cash.

Clearly, it should not be in the form of social programs because such mechanisms are inherently unequal in their application. By reason of age, family circumstances, and a whole variety of other factors, human individual needs are varied and different. Large-scale government social programs, as good as they may be, cannot possibly take these things into account. Most social programs inevitably run contrary to the concept fairness, so by using such instruments in an attempt to restore economic justice, we would be exchanging one form of inequality for another.

Consider, for example, the problem of student loan debt. Currently, there are proposals for the federal government to relieve the borrowers of their burden through federally financed loan forgiveness. Now there are about forty-five million people with outstanding student loan debt who are among the two hundred million adults comprising the four bottom quintiles of the population. Therefore, a program to pay off the outstanding loans could benefit less than 25% of the eligible population. The remaining 75% get nothing. Moreover, the value of individual loans that may qualify for retirement will range from a few hundred dollars to tens of thousands of dollars, so even among the favored minority, there would be wide swings in the distribution of benefits—thus even more inequality.

From this and other examples, I conclude that the only way to assure a fair and equal distribution of benefits is through cash. People will spend or save such redistributive recompense as befits their needs, and in this way and only in this way can the restoration of economic justice be equitably advanced.

CHAPTER THIRTEEN

Conclusion

D O YOU REMEMBER when you were taught in school about the tragic flaw that affected the main character in a play or novel? It appeared frequently in Greek tragedies, like the Oedipus cycle, or in Shakespearean plays (*Macbeth* and *Othello*). The tragic flaw is described as a trait that brings about the downfall of the hero. Often it is the very trait that leads to his success.

Well, capitalism has its own tragic flaw. It is the trait or instinct common to all living things that has been the subject of this book, namely, the compulsion to act first in one's own selfish interests—an act that drives the aspirational motivations making capitalism the most effective way in history to maximize national wealth. But also, it is this same instinct, if not controlled, that can lead to extremes of income and wealth inequality that can become so egregious as to be intolerable to the general population, which, in turn, can cause social and political discord so severe as to imperil the well-being of everyone.

Consider the First World War or the 1917 Russian Revolution. In both instances, the holders of concentrated wealth were cleared out. They died or were exiled in poverty. In 2020, we in the United States are again immersed in such an economic climate, with extreme concentrations of wealth in the hands of a very few while the vast majority stagnates with low incomes, miniscule savings, and little hope. This is a recipe for social disaster with unpredictable outcomes.

The thrust of this book is the coherence of capitalism with Darwinian selfishness, which is the axle around which natural selection revolves. Capitalism's antithesis is socialism, which can function only with the support of an authoritarian structure that chokes off the expression of individual selfishness. Capitalism produces great wealth. It succeeds because of its compatibility with the winnowing principles of evolution. Socialism always fails, not necessarily from the egalitarian nature of many of its social programs but rather because of its incompatibility with these same winnowing principles of evolution.

This raises the question, Is there a middle way? The answer is, of course, there is a middle way, and there are living examples of it.

In China, following the death of Mao, there was a gradual acceptance of capitalist/free market economics. It has been extraordinarily successful, but its success has come at the expense of the egalitarian principles that lie at the core of socialism. Income and wealth inequality in China is among the highest in the world. However, notwithstanding its success, the freely expansive Chinese capitalism of the 1980–2010 period is now being reined in by the self-destructive tendency of socialism toward rigid authoritarian control. This can imperil capitalist initiative. Therefore, only time will tell whether the Chinese experiment represents a middle way that can prevail over the long term.

Better examples of the middle way are the Nordic countries and, to a lesser extent, the Western European countries. So far, these economies have been able to combine income leveling high taxation funding broad-based comprehensive social programs in health care, education, eldercare, etc. with an economic structure that leaves intact the beneficial momentum of innovation and creativity that are the natural product of capitalism. This is working in Europe, and there is no reason why it could not work elsewhere. Therefore, a key finding of this study is that the United States would be well advised to move in this direction. Furthermore, whether voluntary or not, I sense that the social capitalist model of the Nordic countries is inevitable for the United States if it wishes to avoid economic and social chaos.

However, notwithstanding the all-too-obvious advantages of social capitalism, I have observed that for capitalism to function, there must be gradations in income. The utility of these gradations is that they provide step-by-step motivation resulting in innovation, economic growth, and high levels of prosperity. But it is critical to note that while gradations of *income* are central to the capitalist model, gradations in *wealth* are not.

In fact, it may be argued that gradations in wealth and, in particular, concentrations of wealth can be destructive of the capitalist model and equally destructive to democracy. This is because great wealth can buy votes and politicians whose job security is largely dependent on being able to finance their election or reelection campaigns, and in this way, democracy gives way to oligarchy. Democracy becomes illusionary. The real power resides with the uber-rich.

Therefore, while the nation's wealth may be enlarged by the expansion of national income derived from income inequality, the nation's misery is enlarged by its inequitable distribution. So it would seem to be perfectly logical that the redistribution of large pools of concentrated wealth would be beneficial not only insofar as it improves the lives of a majority of people but also insofar as it serves to preserve our democracy. In the short run, this can be achieved by government intervention. One should think of such intervention as being the reverse—the mirror image—of the intervention in favor of the wealthy that occurred over the past forty years through tax and regulatory policies that advantaged the wealthy. In fairness, the funding for such redistribution should take the form of very high taxes on inheritances and very high taxes on concentrated wealth, all or most of which had been accumulated through the generosity of the United States Internal Revenue Service in past years. It would simply be a matter of rebalancing the accounts.

There are strong counterarguments to my suggestion of high inheritance and wealth taxes. It will be argued that not all concentrated wealth is sterile. It forms the foundation for the economy's capital base. Moreover, it will be asserted that accumulated wealth is the primary source of risk capital to fund the economy's innovative technologies.

It does not, however, take a great deal of investigation to see that these arguments come up short. In the first instance, the notion that taxation of accumulated wealth may somehow deplete the store of capital needed to finance business and government is belied by the price of funding. If there is a surplus of a commodity, the price goes down. Well, the price of funding (i.e., interest rates) for business and government has been steadily declining for over twenty years. It is now at an all-time low. There is so much excess capital; there is even talk of negative interest rates. Therefore, the probability that high taxation of accumulated wealth would crowd out private demand would seem to present little risk, especially when measured against the potential gain.

And as for the questions regarding the supply of risk capital to fund the development of new technologies, the facts again belie the myth. It is commonly thought that private investors or venture entities are the source of funds for research and development. This is not so. Accumulated wealth held by individuals or their surrogates almost never invests in new ventures and new technologies at the high-risk stage where technological innovation happens. No, it is the federal government, universities, and nonprofits that do this. In 2017, the federal government provided 42% of the funding for basic research, business provided 30%, and universities, nonprofits, and state governments provided 28%. As for applied research and development, business provides more than 60% of the funding, and it is in the later stages of the development process that private investors participating in venture funds begin to appear, but only to an insignificant degree.[116]

Therefore, given the long-standing and persistent oversupply of capital on a worldwide basis, I think we can safely say that the *de minimis* depletion of capital produced by the taxation of wealth, along with the insignificant reduction in the numbers of risk-averse private investors in early-stage technological R&D, constitutes sufficient countervailing evidence to support the assumption that taxing accumulated wealth will have little or no impact to the availability of funding for government, business, or research and development.

116 Congressional Research Service, *Federal Research and Development Funding (R&D): FY2020*, accessed September 19, 2020, https://fas.org/sgp/crs/misc/R45715.pdf.

Mariana Mazzucato, *The Entrepreneurial State: Debunking Public vs. Private Sector Myths* (New York: Hachette Book Group Inc. 2015), 55.

Evolution

The past few chapters have covered matters regarding inequality. However, the title of this book and its implied purpose is to identify the relationship between economics and evolution, so now let us return to the description of Darwin's theory, as discussed in the first two chapters, and attempt to bring together all the loose threads.

Charles Darwin's theory was fairly simple. From its inception as a single-cell organism (or perhaps as some prelife entity), life evolved in extremely small steps over millions of years into a near countless number of forms. It continues in this process today and will continue into the future. Each miniscule step is the product of a vast number of random mutations that just happen to result in improved fitness of the organism in which it appears.

Fitness is defined as the capacity for survival and reproduction. Mainly it is the product of mutations that occur during cellular division. So a mutation that enables an organism to survive, when retained in the genetic makeup of the organism, would be passed on to future generations. In a similar fashion, if some mutation allow it to reproduce more effectively, then it, too, would be retained and passed on. These changes are called adaptations. Adaptations can be physical, mental, or social, but keep in mind that only a very few, if any, of a species' many mutations will turn out to be fitness-improving adaptations. However, one change that had to occur at the very inception of life was the very first adaptation needed to assure fitness. It is (for lack of a better description) the desire or the drive to live and reproduce. Absent the expressed need to survive and reproduce, there'd be no such thing as life.

It is this compulsion or drive that is the underlying principle of all plant and animal behavior. From single-cell bacteria to tiny insects to trees and garden vegetables and all the way up the hierarchy of life up to and including humans, it is survival and reproduction that directly predetermines virtually all behavior. Only in humans and a few social organisms, such as bees and ants, can it work in an indirect fashion, but even there, it is always operative.

Regarding behavior, and especially human economic behavior, which is nothing more than the acquisition and enhancement of goods and services needed for survival and reproduction, I have encapsulated the drive for survival and reproduction into a single word: *selfishness.*

In this book, I have analyzed the consistency of economic systems and economic behaviors with the fundamental drive of selfishness. To the extent that a system or behavior is consistent with or favorable to the primitive drive of selfishness, it is likely to be more successful than a system or behavior that is in conflict with this underlying principle of life. It is for this reason that I arrive at the conclusion that capitalism, which is built on a foundation of selfishness, will always prevail, while socialism, which requires the suppression of selfishness, will always fail.

However, there is one critical caveat: it is what Darwin called the struggle for life. This is the competition for the fixed resources of a finite planet by reproductively prolific living things. The never-ending interplay of competition and adaptations is what produces the extraordinary variety of life forms, including the human life form. But critically, it also serves as a natural regulator inasmuch as it prevents any one species from getting the upper hand and, in the words of Charles Darwin, "covering the earth with the progeny of a single pair."[117] That is up until the appearance of humans!

Humans, with their superior cognitive capacity, have come to dominate the planet. However, notwithstanding any expectation that their intellect would allow humans to overcome the ultracompetitive tendencies of their ingrained selfishness, human history is one long bloody story of competition, war, and strife. In the economic sphere, the failure to self-regulate or at least place controlling limits on the otherwise deterministic thrust of selfishness is leading to the despoliation of nature and the destruction of its most successful form of socioeconomic organization through the uncontrolled expansion of income and wealth inequality.

---

117 Darwin (2003), 63.

This work, therefore, is nothing if not a call for reason to prevail over determinism. It is my thesis that controlled capitalism fueled by evolutionary determinism is the only way to assure prosperity, but uncontrolled capitalism, or unbounded greed, is the best way to assure universal impoverishment.

APPENDIX A

Additional Considerations Based on the Pandemic of 2020

I N THE MODEL summarized on tables 18 and 19, I have attempted to demonstrate how a return to economic justice can be accomplished by changes to federal income and wealth tax policies. These changes are very substantial. In 2016 (the pro forma year), total federal receipts were approximately $3.3 trillion and individual income taxes were approximately $1.5 trillion. Individual income taxes represented 8.3% of GDP.

In this model, I have proposed $387 billion of increased individual income taxes, bringing the total individual income taxes to $2.1 trillion, or 10% of GDP. In addition, I proposed a new wealth tax of $745 billion, which would represent another 3.6% of GDP. In total, I am proposing a total individual taxes of 13.9% of GDP and total federal receipts of 22.3% of GDP. This would be the highest ratio of federal taxes to GDP on record. The next highest year would be 1944, when the ratio was 20.5%. However, this total increase in annual taxes of $1,132 billion, or 5.0% of GDP, as radical as it may seem, does nothing more than cure the economic injustice done to the middle class over the past forty years.

Unfortunately, there's more to be done, for these tax increases deal only with rectifying a class-based economic injustice. Yet in light of the 2020–2021 coronavirus pandemic, there is a second even more daunting fiscal problem that affects everyone, as the economy is now challenged by the need to fund an emergency comparable in scale to a major war.

The Congressional Budget Office has addressed this matter in a report titled *The 2020 Long-Term Budget Outlook*, issued in September 2020. This report is oriented toward federal debt and interest payments, so the frame of reference appropriate to this analysis, as with all credit analytics, relates to the capacity of the borrower (the United States government) to service its debt.

Before getting into this subject, I must apologize to the reader because I now will be presenting data in a new frame of reference in order to correspond with the CBO study. The CBO data is configured not as absolute numbers but rather as a relationship, expressed as the percent debt to GDP. This the best and most commonly used method for discussing information of this type, but I must admit it can be a bit confusing. For example, the 2019 ratio of debt to GDP was 79%, and the estimate for 2020 is 98%.[118] At the same time, the record shows that over the past twenty years, the federal tax receipts as a percent of GDP have fluctuated between 15 and 18% and have been closer to 18% in recent years.[119] So for example, if the debt is 100% of GDP and the tax receipts are 18% of GDP, then the ratio of debt to revenue is 5.5×. Although it is not precisely analogous, it may help to think of this ratio as being similar to the ratio a mortgage lender uses when he tells you that the maximum you can borrow is limited to four or five times your annual income. Of course, the same limitations do not apply to the United States Treasury, but the credit analysis is roughly the same. It's simply a shorthand way to describe the relationship of debt to the carrying capacity of the borrower. I hope this short example helps. So now with this background, let us see what the CBO data reveals.

As noted above, the CBO analysis shows a starting level of debt to GDP at 79% at the beginning of 2020. This is very high. Some would say that it is irresponsibly high because it leaves little room to

---

118 Congressional Budget Office, *The 2020 Long-Term Budget Outlook* (September 2020), 8, table 1, accessed September 25, 2020, www.cbo.gov/publications/56516.
119 Office of Management and Budget, "Historical Tables: Table 2.3—Receipts by Source as Percentages of GDP: 1934–2025," accessed September 25, 2020, www.whitehouse.gov/omb.

accommodate emergencies or unexpected crises.[120] I would agree, and reading between the lines, so does the CBO.

The CBO long-term budget outlook projects the government's receipts, expenditures, deficits, and national debt out to 2050. Assuredly, this kind of a forecast can deal with the future only in broad strokes. It is constructed to draw out implications for the future based on the policies and programs of the present. Therefore, among the important assumptions are (1) that current laws affecting revenues and spending remain unchanged and (2) that existing programs such as Medicare, Medicaid, and various welfare benefits continue even beyond their possible expiration dates or the exhaustion of their trust funds. Essentially, this forecast answers the question, What happens if we do nothing to fix the fiscal problems? But also, it makes no allowance for the probable effects of cyclical downturns, possible wars, or other emergencies requiring extra funding. As the projection builds over time, it's on autopilot and predicts certain inevitable phenomena such as (1) deficits in every year, (2) rising federal debt and a constantly increasing ratio of federal debt to GDP, (3) higher-accumulated interest costs to both the federal and private sectors, especially in the out-years, and (4) declining rate of increase in GDP due to a growing weakness of the debt markets to service private investment needs as federal issuances crowd

---

120 The debt of the United States government held by the public in 1980, when Ronald Reagan assumed the presidency, was **25.5% of GDP**. During the next eight years, it **rose to 39.9% of GDP**. Under George Bush, it **went up to 46.8%** of GDP. Then under Bill Clinton, it **declined to 33.7% of GDP.** Following Clinton's years of superb budget management, it then **rose to 39.4% of GDP** under George W. Bush. This led to the Obama years when extremely poor budget management, unprecedented in peacetime, took the nation's debt as a percent of GDP **up to 76.4%**. This was followed by Trump's equally bad budget management that by the end of 2020 will have taken the debt **up to 98.2% of GDP**. Both Obama and Trump experienced the bad luck of having to manage through a crisis in GDP, but neither did anything to offset it. Both acted irresponsibly in putting the nation into such a precarious position. Obama because he increased spending without increasing taxes, and Trump because he decreased taxes without decreasing spending. The result, as the CBO clearly demonstrates, prefigures hard times ahead.

out the private sector and reduce the supply of funds. The following table summarizes the salient points.

Table 20. Key Projections in the CBO'S Extended Baseline Forecast

	2020	Annual Average 2021–2030	Annual Average 2031–2040	Annual Average 2041–2050
GDP at End of Period (Trillions)	$20.6	$30.7	$43.8	$62.0
Primary Deficit (% of GDP)	(14.4)%	(3.5)%	(3.7)%	(6.5)%
Net Interest (% of GDP)	(1.6)%	(1.5)%	(3.8)%	(4.4)%
Annual Deficit (% of GDP)	**(16.0)%**	**(5.0)%**	**(7.5)%**	**(10.9)%**
Debt Held by the Public at the End of Period (% of GDP)	**98%**	**109%**	**142%**	**195%**
Reference: Annual Average Debt Held by the Public 1979–2019 (% of GDP)	48%	48%	48%	48%

Source: Congressional Budget Office, *The 2020 Long-Term Budget Outlook*, 8.

From this data, it should be perfectly clear that the current economic situation, if not corrected, puts the nation on an exceedingly risky path. The very idea that federal debt as a percent of GDP should exceed 100%, trending toward 195%, positions the United States in the select company of such paragons of fiscal integrity as Venezuela (214%),

Greece (178%), Lebanon (158%), and Italy(133%). It also positions us with Japan (238%), which is the leader of the pack. But unlike the United States and most other nations, Japan's condition is substantially different because its debt is entirely held by its own citizens, which makes its liquidation or monetization somewhat less traumatic, whereas for the United States, 39% of its debt is held by foreigners.

Debt ratios this high are uncharted territory. No one really knows the implications; however, some of the concerns are (1) exposure to the crippling cost of interest rates higher than the 4% built into the later years of the forecast, (2) increased vulnerability to domestic and foreign policy from foreign owners of Treasury securities, (3) market risk of refinancing, potentially leading to a depression-like fiscal crisis, (4) possible stimulus to hyperinflation, (5) inability to readily finance in response to national security threats, (6) crowding out private borrowers from the financial markets, leading to reduced investment and diminished GDP, and (7) loss of the nation's status as the world's reserve currency. These are but a few of the risks to the nation posed by an extraordinarily high ratio of debt to GDP. Nothing good can come of this.

The whole purpose of the CBO analysis was not simply to identify the problem and inescapable consequences of high federal debt but also to demonstrate the unavoidable costs associated with extracting the economy from this difficulty. And the costs are, indeed, high.

The CBO estimates that reducing the debt level in 2050 to the 2019 level of 79% of GDP will require that the annual deficit beginning in 2025 and going forward must be reduced by 3.6% of GDP, which in 2025 is a reduction of $900 billion.[121] As GDP grows in subsequent years, the annual dollar amount will also grow. This will necessitate a severe cut in discretionary programs or the imposition of much higher taxes.

In the model summarized earlier in this chapter, I showed how such higher taxes could be attained without imperiling the dynamics of our economic system by sourcing taxes from wealth rather than income.

---

121 CBO (2020), 16.

Such an approach is, in my opinion, the only rational solution to the problem so clearly defined by the CBO. And there is certainly the opportunity for more revenues. For example, in the earlier discussion of estate/inheritance taxation, I noted Lily Batchelder's plan may yield $34 billion in pro forma annual revenues, but she also demonstrated within her proposed structure that by decreasing the exemption from $2.5 million to $500,000, the annual inheritance tax revenues could be increased from $34 billion to $140 billion without even increasing the underlying effective tax rate.

APPENDIX B

The Minimum Wage as a Partial Solution

I T HAS BEEN suggested that increasing the minimum wage should be the first step to correct imbalances in income distribution. According to the United States Bureau of Labor Statistics (BLS), in 2018, there were approximately 1.7 million workers earning the federal minimum wage of $7.25 per hour. In 1979, the federal minimum wage was $2.90 per hour. Adjusting the 1979 wage rate for cost of living would mean that on inflation adjustment alone, the federal minimum wage in 2018 should have been $10.03. Then adjusting this rate by the compound annual growth rate (CAGR) of real wages for the period 1979–2018, which was approximately 1.45%, would produce a minimum wage of $17.58. This would be an $10.33 increase over the current rate.

In terms of households (the unit of measure used in the tables on chapter 12), the 1.7 million workers equate to about 708,000 households. Multiplying this figure by the $10.33 increase in wages and the product of this by 1,604 average hours worked by minimum-wage workers in 2018 would yield an improvement in aggregate wages of about $10.7 billion.

This is not an insignificant number. Remember, the minimum amount needed to correct the income injustice done to all but the top 1.0% since 1979 is approximately $860 billion per year; the increase in the minimum wage could contribute about 1.2% of the need. Of course, that is before taking into account the inevitable layoffs and acceleration of the employer's replacement of human workers by automation. My guess is that the net yield would more likely be half of the calculated number. Nevertheless, for the wage earner, it is significant. And for the economy, it is the right thing to do.

ACKNOWLEDGMENTS

I N RECENT YEARS, a new genre of economists have emerged. Unlike previous generations who most frequently developed theories and policy recommendations based on the elegance of formulas detached from reality, this generation starts with voluminous data and grounds its work on the facts.

For empiricists, like myself, this has been like a breath of fresh air. It gives great hope that policymakers will finally be well served by the profession. No more Laffer Curves, aggregate propensities to consume, and above all, no more trickle-down.

One of the most important developments has been the generosity of scholars in sharing the detailed evidence that they use to support their published reports and books. They do this with online appendixes. I cannot help but believe that such broad and unconstrained dissemination of the data will most certainly result in better informed economic analysis and, ultimately, better public policy.

Organizations such as the Congressional Budget Office, the Federal Reserve, the World Bank, the Organisation for Economic Co-operation and Development, and the International Monetary Fund are among those whose databases independent scholars such as myself are privileged to access. Academic institutions and think tanks such as the Paris School of Economics, the Groningen Growth and Development Centre, the Brookings Institution, and the National Bureau of Economic Research are likewise generous with their data resources. And, of course, there are many excellent scholars working in this field. In addition to those at the aforementioned institutions, I would like to acknowledge the following authors, without whose published insights this work would have not been possible: Lily Batchelder, Branko Milanovic, Thomas Piketty, Emmanuel Saez, and Gabriel Zucman.

I would also like to thank my friend Ed Kennedy for his many suggestions. And I especially wish to thank Thomas Devlin, one of

America's preeminent biochemists whose text on biochemistry was a staple of most medical schools for many decades, for his gracious help. Tom read and commented not only on the sections regarding biology but also on the structure of the argument and nature of the social and economic analysis.

Of course, it goes without saying that any and all errors, misinterpretation of source work, or misuse of data are entirely my own fault.

Finally, I would like to say that this work, as well as everything else I have done in life, would have been impossible without the love and support of my wife, Diane. She started before we were married, typing my papers in graduate school, and now, nearly sixty years later, she is still hard at work correcting my mistakes and proofreading my papers. In this, as in all else, she is my constant support and best friend.

BIBLIOGRAPHY

Arnhart, Larry. *Darwinian Natural Right: The Biological Ethics of Human Nature*. Albany: The State University of New York Press, 1998.

Bagnall, Roger S., ed. *Egypt in the Byzantine World*. Cambridge: Cambridge University Press, 2013.

Batchelder, Lily. "Leveling the Playing Field between Inherited Income and Income from Work through an Inheritance Tax." In *Tackling the Tax Code: Efficient and Equitable Ways to Raise Revenue*, edited by Jay Shambaugh and Ryan Nunn. Washington, DC: The Hamilton Project, 2020.

Berle, Adolf A., Jr., and Gardiner C. Means. *The Modern Corporation and Private Property*. New York: The Macmillan Company, 1932.

Berle, Adolf A., Jr. *Power without Property: A New Development in American Political Economy*. New York: Harcourt, Brace and Company, 1959.

Blinder, Alan S. "The Anatomy of Double Digit Inflation." In *Inflation: Causes and Effects*, edited by Robert E. Hall, 261–282. Chicago: University of Chicago Press, 1982.

Bolt, Jutta, Robert Inklaar, Herman deJong, and Jan Luiten van Zanden. "Rebasing Maddison: New Income Comparisons and the Shape of Long-Run Economic Development, Maddison Project Working Paper 10." *Maddison Project Database, Version 2018*. Groningen Growth and Development Centre, University of Groningen, 2018.

Boushey, Heather. *Unbound: How Inequality Constricts Our Economy and What We Can Do About It*. Cambridge, MA: Harvard University Press, 2019.

Bowman, Alan, and Andrew Wilson, eds. *Quantifying the Roman Economy*. Oxford: Oxford University Press, 2009.

Braudel, Fernand. *Civilization and Capitalism, Volume I*. Translated by Sian Reynolds. New York: Harper & Row Publishers Inc., 1981.

Buckley, Chris. "Xi Doctrine Will Guide a Nation." *New York Times*, February 27, 2018, section A, page 8, New York edition.

Carrol, Sean B. *The Making of the Fittest*. New York: W. W. Norton & Company, 2007.

Chauveau, Michel. *Egypt in the Age of Cleopatra*. Translated by David Lorton. Ithaca: Cornell University Press, 2000.

Congressional Budget Office. *The Distribution of Household Income, 2016*. Washington, DC: March 2018.

Darwin, Charles. *The Origin of Species*. New York: Penguin Group, 2003.

Darwin, Charles. *Voyage of the Beagle*. London: Penguin Books Ltd., 1989.

Davis, James B., et al. *The Level and Distribution of Household Wealth*. Cambridge, MA: National Bureau of Economic Research, 2009.

Dawkins, Richard. *The Extended Phenotype*. Oxford: Oxford University Press, 1999.

Dawkins, Richard. *The Selfish Gene, 40th Anniversary Edition*. Oxford: Oxford University Press, 2006.

Devlin, Thomas M., ed. *Textbook of Biochemistry: With Clinical Correlations.* New York: John Wiley & Sons Inc., 2011.

Dorn, James A. *The Genesis and Evolution of China's Economic Liberalization.* Cato Working Paper No. 38. Washington, DC: The Cato Institute, 2016.

Easterly, William, and Stanley Fischer. "The Soviet Economic Decline: Historical and Republican Data." *World Bank Policy Working Paper 1284.* 1994.

Economy, Elizabeth C. "The Great Firewall of China: Xi Jinping's Internet Shutdown." *The Guardian*, June 29, 2018.

Finley, M. I. *The Ancient Economy.* Berkeley: University of California Press, 1999.

Finneran, Niall. *Alexandria, a City and Myth.* Stroud, UK: Tempus, 2005.

Friedman, George. "The Truth about the US-China Thucydides Trap." *Geopolitical Futures,* July 14, 2020.

Gaidor, Yegor. *Collapse of an Empire: Lessons for Modern Russia.* Translated by Antonina Bous. Washington, DC: Brookings Institute Press, 2007.

Garbinti, Bertrand, Jonathon Goupille-Lebret, and Thomas Piketty. *Income Inequality in France: Economic Growth and Gender Gap.* London: Center for Economic and Policy Research, 2020.

Gintis, Herbert. *Individuality and Entanglement: The Moral and Material Bases of Social Life.* Princeton: Princeton University Press, 2017.

Giovannoni, Olivier. *What Do We Know about Labor Share and Profit Share?* Annandale-On-Hudson, NY: Levy Economics Institute, 2014.

Grant, Michael. *History of Rome.* New York: Charles Scribner's Sons, 1978.

Greer, Tanner. "Xi Jinping in Translation: China's Guiding Ideology." *Palladium Magazine,* May 31, 2019.

Gue, Martin. *Soviet Economic Growth 1928–1985.* Los Angeles: RAND Center for the Study of Soviet Economic Behavior, 1988.

Haas, Christopher. *Alexandria in Late Antiquity, Topography and Social Conflict.* Baltimore: John Hopkins University Press, 1997.

Hayek, Friedrich A. *The Road to Serfdom.* Chicago: The University of Chicago Press, 1958.

Hill, Christopher. *The Pelican Economic History of Britain, Volume 2, 1530 to 1780, Reformation to Industrial Revolution.* New York: Viking-Penguin, 1986.

Hobsbawm, E. J. *Industry and Empire.* New York: Viking-Penguin Inc., 1987.

Hodgson, Geoffrey M. *Evolutionary Economics: Its Nature and Future.* Cambridge: Cambridge University Press, 2019.

Horden, Peregrine, and Nicholas Purcell. *The Corrupting Sea, a Study of Mediterranean History.* Oxford: Blackwell Publishers Inc., 2000.

Huifeng, He. "How Does China's Social Credit System Work?" *South China Morning Post,* February 18, 2019.

Johnson, Calvin H. "A Wealth Tax Is Constitutional," *ABA Tax Times* 38, no. 4 (Summer 2019). Chicago: American Bar Association.

Johnson, Gale D. "The Functional Distribution of Income in the United States, 1850–1953." In *The Review of Economics and Statistics* 36, no. 2 (1954). doi: 102307/1924668.

Karabarbounis, Loukas, and Brent Neiman. *The Global Decline in Labor Share*. NBER Working Paper 19136. Cambridge, MA: National Bureau of Economic Research, 2013.

Lane, Nick. *The Vital Question: Energy, Evolution, and the Origins of Complex Life*. New York: W. W. Norton & Company Inc., 2016.

Lansford, Thomas. *Communism*. New York: Cavendish Square Publishing, 2007.

Majerus, Michael, William Amos, and George Hurst. *Evolution: The Four Billion Year War*. Essex, UK: Addison Wesley Longman Limited, 1996.

Manning, Joseph G. "Water, Irrigation, and their Connection to State Power in Egypt." 2012. Unpublished manuscript issued at www.econ.yale.edu/egcenter/manning-2012pdy.

Mazat, Numa, and Franklin Serrano. *An Analysis of Soviet Growth from the 1950's to the Collapse of the USSR*. Accessed April 1, 2020. www.centrostaffa.org/public/bb6a675-6bef-4182-bb89-39ae1f7e792.pdf.

Mazzucato, Mariana. *The Entrepreneurial State*. New York: Hachette Book Group Inc., 2018.

Milanovic, Branko. *Capitalism, Alone: The Future of the System that Rules the World*. Cambridge, MA: Harvard University Press, 2019.

Miller, Kenneth R. *The Human Instinct: How We Evolved to Have Reason, Consciousness and Free Will.* New York: Simon and Schuster, 2018.

Mistreamu, Simina. "Life within China's Social Credit Laboratory." *Foreign Policy,* April 3, 2018.

Mokyr, Joel. *The Lever of Riches: Technological Creativity and Economic Progress.* New York: Oxford University Press, 1990.

Nelson, Richard R., ed. *Modern Evolutionary Economics.* Cambridge: Cambridge University Press, 2018.

Organisation for Economic Co-operation and Development (OECD). "The Labour Share in G20 Economies, Report Prepared for the G20 Employment Working Group, Anatalya, Turkey, 26–27 February 2015."

Owens, E. J. *The City in the Greek and Roman World.* London: Routledge, 1992.

Owen, Robert Dale. *Threading My Way: Twenty-Seven Years of Autobiography.* London: Trübner & Co., 1874.

Pei, Minxin. "China's Coming Upheaval: Competition, the Coronavirus, and the Weakness of Xi Jinping." In *Foreign Affairs* 99, no. 3 (May/June 2020): 82–95.

Piketty, Thomas. *Capital and Ideology.* Translated by Arthur Goldhammer. Cambridge, MA: Harvard University Press, 2020.

Piketty, Thomas. *Capital in the Twenty-First Century.* Translated by Arthur Goldhammer. Cambridge, MA: Harvard University Press, 2014.

Piketty, Thomas, Emmanuel Saez, and Gabriel Zucmam. "Distribution of National Accounts: Methods and Estimates for the United States." *The Quarterly Journal of Economics* 133, no. 2 (May 2018): 553–609.

Pinker, Steven. *Enlightenment Now: The Case for Reason, Science, Humanism, and Progress*. New York: Viking-Penguin, 2018.

Polanyi, Karl. *The Great Transformation*. Boston: Beacon Press, 1960.

Reich, David. *Who We Are and How We Got There: Ancient DNA and the New Science of the Human Past*. New York: Penguin Random House LLC., 2018.

Ridley, Matt. *Genome: The Autobiography of a Species in 23 Chapters*. New York: HarperCollins Publishers, 2007.

Rostovtzeff, M. *The Social and Economic History of the Hellenistic World*. London: Oxford University Press, 1941.

Saez, Emmanuel, and Gabriel Zucman. *The Triumph of Injustice: How the Rich Dodge Taxes and How to Make Them Pay*. New York: W. W. Norton & Company, 2019.

Saez, Emmanuel, and Gabriel Zicmam. *Wealth Inequality in the United States since 1913: Evidence from Capitalized Income Tax Data*. NBER Working Paper 20625. Cambridge, MA: National Bureau of Economic Research, 2014.

Sarin, Natasha, Lawrence A. Summers, and Joel Kupferberg. *Tax Reform for Progressivity: A Pragmatic Approach*. Washington, DC: The Hamilton Project, January 28, 2020.

Sawyer, G. J., Victor Deak, and Esteban Sarmiento. *The Last Human: A Guide to Twenty-Two Species of Extinct Humans*. New Haven: Yale University Press, 2009.

Scheidel, Walter, and Steven J. Friesen. "The Size of the Economy and the Distribution of Income in the Roman Economy." *The Journal of Roman Studies* 99 (2009): 61–91.

Scheidel, Walter. *Escape from Rome: The Failure of Empire and the Road to Prosperity*. Princeton: Princeton University Press, 2019.

Scheidel, Walter. *The Great Leveler, Violence and the History of Inequality*. Princeton: Princeton University Press, 2017.

Schleifer, Andrei, and Robert W. Vishny. "Reversing the Soviet Economic Collapse." *Brookings Papers on Economic Activity, 2*. 1991.

Schumpeter, Joseph A. *Capitalism, Socialism and Democracy*. New York: HarperCollins Publishers, 2008.

Service, Robert. *Comrades: A History of World Communism*. Cambridge, MA: Harvard University Press, 2007.

Stambough, John E. *The Ancient Roman City*. Baltimore: The Johns Hopkins University Press, 1988.

Starr, Chester G. *A History of the Ancient World*. New York: Oxford University Press, 1991.

Stone, Chad, Danilo Trisi, Arloc Sherman, and Jennifer Beltrain. *A Guide to Statistics on Historical Trends in Income Inequality*. Washington, DC: Center on Budget and Policy Priorities, 2020.

Temin, Peter. *The Roman Market Economy*. Princeton: Princeton University Press, 2013.

Theilhard de Chardin, Pierre. *The Phenomenon of Man*. Translated by Bernard Wall. New York: Harper Brothers Publishers, 1959.

Wapshott, Nicholas. *Keynes Hayek: The Clash that Defined Modern Economics*. New York: W. W. Norton & Company, 2011.

Ward-Perkins, Bryan. *The Fall of Rome and the End of Civilization*. Oxford: Oxford University Press, 2006.

Watson, James D. *DNA: The Story of the Genetic Revolution*. New York: Alfred A. Knopf, 2017.

Weitzman, Martin. "Soviet Postwar Economic Growth and Capital Labor Substitution." *American Economic Review* 60 (1970).

West, Geoffrey. *Scale: The Universal Laws of Life, Growth, and Death in Organisms, Cities, and Companies*. New York: Penguin Random House LLC, 2017.

Wilson, David Sloan. *This View of Life: Completing the Darwinian Revolution*. New York: Penguin Random House LLC, 2019.

Wilson, Edward O. *The Meaning of Human Existence*. New York: W. W. Norton & Company Inc., 2014.

Wilson, W. B. "Extract from the Report of the President's Mediation Commission." In *American Industry in the War: A Report of the War Industries Board* by Bernard Baruch. Transmitted March 3, 1921. New York: Prentice-Hall, 1941.

Wolff, Edward N. *Household Wealth in the United States, 1962 to 2016; Has Middle Class Wealth Recovered?* NBER Working Paper 24085. Cambridge, MA: National Bureau of Economic Research, 2017.

Wood, Tony. "Organization over Ideals: The Global History of the Communist Party." *The Nation*, March 25, 2019.

World Inequality Lab at the Paris School of Economics. *World Inequality Report 2018*. Paris: Paris School of Economics, 2019.

Zakaria, Fareed. "The New China Scare: Why America Shouldn't Panic About Its Latest Challenger." *Foreign Affairs* 99 no. (January/ February 2020): 52–69.

INDEX

A

adaptations, 17, 20, 22, 158
adenine, thymine, cytosine, and guanine (ATCG), 11
adenosine triphosphate (ATP), 9
Alexander the Great, 34n24
Alexandria, 34n24, 174
altruism, xviii
annona, 35
anti-corruption campaign, 103–4, 106, 110
authoritarian system, 27, 29–31, 33–34
Avery, Oswald, 10

B

bacteria, 14
Batchelder, Lily, 147–48, 166, 169, 171
Berle, Adolf, 85–86, 171
Bolsheviks, 50
Borlaug, Norman, 123
bourgeoisie, 48
Braudel, Fernand, 33, 172
British Navigation Acts, 70

C

capital, 55–56, 88–90, 157, 176, 179
    depreciation, 94
    mobility, 149
capitalism, xii, xxi–xxii, 49, 69, 74, 76, 80, 86, 99, 101–2, 113, 121–23, 129–30, 154–55, 159–60
    and aspirational motivation, 130, 150
    and its self-destructive defects, xxii
    and profit, 69–70, 174

growth mechanism, 70
structure, 71
types
    liberal meritocratic, 80–81, 85, 87, 89–91, 99–100
    core assumptions, 99
    nineteenth-century classical, 74, 81, 86, 89
    political, 100, 105, 112, 117
    social democratic, 81–82, 87, 89, 131
    wealth and economic progress, 71
Cheka, 51
China, xxii, 49n34, 66–68, 82–84, 100–105, 108–12, 114–17, 121, 155, 173–74, 176, 180
    2019 Gini coefficient, 68
    Gini coefficient under socialism, 67
Chinese Communist Party (CCP), 102, 104–6, 108
chromosomes, 7, 12
Clayton Act, 73
Cold War, 65, 75
Manifesto, The (Marx and Engels), 47
compound annual growth rate (CAGR), xiv, 127–28, 133, 137, 167
Congressional Budget Office (CBO), 94, 132, 162–63, 166, 169, 172
    The 2020 Long-Term Budget Outlook, 162
constant dollars, xii, 126
consumer price index (CPI), 122
Crick, Francis, 11
Cuba, 54, 75

D

Darwin, Charles, 158
  natural selection, xvii, xx, 3–4, 12–13, 17, 20, 22, 124, 154
    struggle for existence. *See* Darwin, Charles: struggle for life
  struggle for life, 1–2, 19, 124, 159
    survival of the fittest. *See* Darwin, Charles: natural selection
  theory of evolution, xx, 16
    response of Christian community, 5
de Chardin, Pierre Teilhard, xxi
deoxyribonucleic acid (DNA), 10–12, 14–16, 177, 179
  fern, 15
  human, 15
"Distribution of National Accounts: Methods and Estimates for the United States" (Piketty, Saez, and Zucman), 93–94

E

Easterly, William, 56
Eastern Empire, 34
E. coli, 14
economic behavior, xix, 18, 28, 159, 174
Egypt, 28–35, 37, 171–72, 175
Ehrlich, Paul, 123
  The Population Bomb, 123
Engels, Friedrich, 47–48, 49n34, 50, 123
estate tax, 147
Europe, 47, 71, 86–87, 123, 155
eusociality, 20
evolution, xviii–xxi, 7, 16–17, 158, 173, 175
  of intellect, 20
evolutionary change, 16–17
extrapolation, 123–24
extrapolative reasoning, 123

F

factors of production, 72
Fischer, Stanley, 56, 173
France, 41, 90, 173
free markets, xix, 70, 80, 101, 115
Friedman, George, 117

G

Gaidar, Yegor, 57–58, 65
GDP Per Capita, 41
genes, 6–7, 11–12, 15–16
genetics, xix
genetic variety, 3
Gini coefficient, 40, 63, 67–68, 127
  rank of countries, 41
golden age, xiv
Gorbachev, Mikhail, 54, 58
government intervention, 156
gradations, 129, 142, 150, 155–56
Great Depression, xiv, 49n34, 87, 90
Great Firewall, 107, 173
Great Society, xiv, 127
greed. *See* selfishness
Green Revolution, 123
Gur, Martin, 56

H

Haemophilius influenzae, 15
helix, 11n9
Herodotus, 32
Homo sapiens, 28
household, 127
household income, 42, 92, 94, 125, 127–28, 139, 141
Human Genome Project, 15

I

inequality, 124
  cure to, 153
  dangers of, 125

income and wealth, 38, 40, 89, 99,
124–25, 129, 137–38, 154–56,
159, 173, 178
Injustice, 113, 134, 137, 147, 161, 167,
177
Interstate Commerce Act, 73
inundation, 30n21, 32

J

Jericho, 28
Jinping, Xi, 83–84, 103–11, 114–17,
172–74, 176
and China's path of socialism, 116
doctrine, 110–11, 172
early life, 109
internet sovereignty, 106
marks of facism, 111–12
severe censorship, 106
social credit system, 107–8, 174
speech on socialism, 114
surveillance technology, 107

L

labor, 72–73, 88, 97, 174–75, 179
and technological change, 88
labor-capital ratio, 87, 90
Lenin, Vladimir, 50–51
livinG tHinGS, 8, 14, 16, 154

M

Marx, Karl, 47–48, 50, 123
Maslyukov, Yuri, 58, 61
Means, Gardiner, 85, 171
meeting transcript (September 17, 1990),
59
Memphis, 33
Mendel, Gregor, 5–7, 15
mercantilism, 70, 80
middle way, 155
Miescher, Friedrich, 10

Milanovic, Branko, 81, 87, 89–93,
95–96, 99–100, 102–3, 112, 117,
169, 175
minimum wage, increasing, 167
mitochondria, 9
*Modern Corporation and Private Property,
The* (Berle and Means), 85, 171
Morgan, Thomas Hunt, 7, 10
The Mechanism of Mendelian Heredity,
7
mutations, 3–4, 16, 158

N

national income, 88, 94
1929, *xiv*
National Labor Relations Act, 87
nematodes, 15
New Deal, 86
New Economic Plan (NEP), 51
New Harmony, 46–47
Nile River, 31
1979, *xiv*
Nordic countries, 41–42, 131, 155
North America, 45–47, 71

O

Occam's razor, xvii
organic model, 27–32
Organisation for Economic Co-
operation and Development
(OECD), 83–84, 176
GDP per capita of countries, 84
Owen, Robert, 46
Owen, Robert Dale, 46

P

Pei, Minxin, 116–17
photosynthesis, 13–14
Poor Law Amendment of 1834, *72*
Population Bomb, The (Ehrlich), 123
prokaryotes, 13–14

proletariat, 47–49
Pure Food and Drug Act, 73

Q

quantitative concepts, xii

R

Reagan-Thatcher revolution, 122
red blood cells, 12, 15
redistribution, aggressive, 138
repressed inflation, 56–57
reproductive cycle, 16–17
Rome, 29–31, 34, 34n24, 34–35, 35n25,
    36–37, 174, 178–79
  trading, 35–36
Russia, 49–54, 57, 59, 120–21, 173
Russian Revolution, 49, 154
Ryabyev, 58
Ryzhkov, Nikolay, 58

S

Scheidel, Walter, 63
selfishness, xii, xvii–xviii, xx–xxi, xxin3,
    xxii, 10, 12–16, 18, 50, 80, 113,
    118, 129–30, 154–55, 159–60
  absence of, xx, 2, 118
Shakers, 47
Sherman Antitrust Act, 73
Shleifer, Andrei, 56
Sitarian, 58
socialism, xii, xxii, 30–31, 45, 47, 49–50,
    52–53, 62, 64–66, 69–70, 74–76,
    113–16, 118–19, 121, 154–55
  and oppression, 66
  monastic life, 45
  negative effects, xiv, 64–65, 119
  Soviet Union and China parallel, 66
  utopian communities, 45–46
socialization. *See* socialism
social programs, 153, 155
somatic, definition of, 15n13

Soviet Union, 53–56, 61–63, 65–66, 75,
    119–20
  average income under socialist rule, 66
  costs of socialism, 64
  Gini coefficient (1968–1985), 63
stagflation, 121
Starr, Chester, 28
state-owned enterprises (SOEs), 101, 115
survival and reproduction, xii, xvii–xix,
    8, 10, 12, 14, 19, 23, 31, 99, 112–
    13, 118, 158–59
Sutton, Walter, 7

T

Taxation of Wealth, 148, 150–51, 157
  difficulties experienced with, 149
Tax Cuts and Jobs Act (TCJA), 146
Temin, Peter, 36
tragic flaw, 154
transfer payments, 40n29
TVEs, 101
2020 Long-Term Budget Outlook, The
  (CBO), 162

U

United States, 42, 73, 83–84, 86, 90,
    100, 121–22, 127, 131–32, 138–
    39, 148, 155, 175, 177, 179
  government debt history, 163n121

V

Vishny, Robert, 56
Voronin, 58

W

wealth
  accumulated, 122, 156–57
  concentrated, 97, 154, 156
Weitzman, Martin, 55
West, Geoffrey, 130

Western Empire, 34, 38
Who's Who of the percentiles, 140–41
Wilson, E. O., 20–22, 172, 179
Wolf, Edward N., 92

X

Xiaoping, Deng, 67, 100, 105
  policies, 105

Z

Zedong, Mao, 66–67, 83, 105–7, 111